THE
HARRY CARAY'S RESTAURANT
COOKBOOK

THE
HARRY CARAY'S RESTAURANT
COOKBOOK

JANE & MICHAEL STERN

RUTLEDGE HILL PRESS™

Nashville, Tennessee

A DIVISION OF THOMAS NELSON, INC.

www.ThomasNelson.com

Published by Rutledge Hill Press, a Division of Thomas Nelson, Inc., P.O. Box 141000, Nashville, Tennessee, 37214.

Library of Congress Cataloging-in-Publication Data

Stern, Jane.
　　The Harry Caray's restaurant cookbook/Jane & Michael Stern.
　　　　p. cm.
　　Includes index.
　　1-4016-0095-6 (hardcover)
　　1. Cookery—Illinois—Chicago. 2. Harry Caray (Restaurant) I. Stern, Michael, 1946– II. Title.
　TX714.S7727 2003
　641.59773'11—dc21   2003003843

Printed in the United States of America

03 04 05 06 07—5 4 3 2 1

Contents

Foreword   vii

Acknowledgments   ix

Introduction   xi

SOUPS   5

SALADS   19

SANDWICHES   35

APPETIZERS   47

SIDE DISHES   67

SAUCES, STOCKS & DRESSINGS   79

PASTA & RISOTTO   101

ITALIAN FAVORITES   127

SEAFOOD   135

CHICKEN   147

STEAKS, VEAL & CHOPS   161

DESSERTS   183

Glossary   197

Index   203

Foreword

As the wife of Harry Caray, I have traveled all over the country, have met many wonderful people, and have had countless new and interesting experiences. One of the experiences that has proven most fulfilling for me is my involvement in Harry Caray's Restaurant. When the developers first came to Harry with the idea for the restaurant, it never occurred to me that it would come to play such a large role in my life. Since Harry's passing, the torch has been handed to me to represent the restaurant to the public. I was a bit hesitant about taking on the role at first, but I've become so involved in the restaurant and with the wonderful people who run it, that it is now second nature to talk about all the great things we're doing. I've been on local and national television speaking about events and promotions at the restaurant more times than I can count. One of those times I was at the restaurant at three o'clock in the morning, wearing a kimono while watching the historic Cubs home opener in Japan! During the Seventh Inning Stretch, I led a bar full of people in singing "Take me out the Ball Game," which was aired live on FOX Sports Channel all throughout the country. Who would have thought?

Many of our customers come to the restaurant for the first time to see what all the excitement is about, but they keep coming back because our food is terrific. The restaurant has become a second home for me, and I eat there at least four times a week with friends and family. I love the food, and I also love the lively, yet comforting, atmosphere that we've created. I am so excited about this cookbook because it gives us a new way to share our great food and interesting stories with even more people. It also finally gives me the chance to make some of my favorite dishes from the restaurant at home.

Jane and Michael Stern have done a wonderful job of capturing the essence of the restaurant as well as the quality of our food in the pages of this cookbook. I urge you to read the many stories and facts that they have sprinkled throughout the book. They provide a great peek into Harry's life and into Chicago—the city he loved so much. Stop by Harry's the next time you're in town. Holy Cow!

— Dutchie Caray

Acknowledgments

We never met Harry Caray, but we sure got to know him well, thanks to all of those people at the restaurant who so lovingly sustain his character. Beth Goldberg Heller ensured that this project was up and running from the start; she and Grant DePorter made us feel welcome in the dining room and helped us see the big picture; Executive Chef Garrick Dickie gave us an eye-opening view of his magnificent kitchen. We are especially grateful to Dutchie Caray for sharing her memories with us over a never-to-be-forgotten lunch.

Our eating partners at *www.roadfood.com* accompany us in spirit and in appetite wherever we go. As we ate our way through the menu at this grand Chicago steakhouse, we raised a virtual toast (Bud, of course) to Steve Rushmore Sr., Stephen Rushmore and Kristin Little, Cindy Keuchle, and Marc Bruno. We are grateful for their indomitable companionship in the quest to find and document America's best food.

Our long-held belief in the glories of American regional cuisine has found such a satisfying expression in this series of books from the nation's most beloved restaurants. Larry Stone, Geoff Stone, Bryan Curtis, Roger Waynick, and Mike Alday are steady reminders that the Roadfood cookbooks reflect a part of America's culture that is well worth celebrating. Their steady stream of good ideas and support has made publishing a pleasure.

As always, we tip our hats in thanks to agent Doe Coover for her tireless work on our behalf, as well as to Jean Wagner, Mary Ann Rudolph, and Ned Schankman for making it possible for us to travel in confidence that all's well at home.

Introduction

HARRY CARAY'S restaurant offers an opportunity to enjoy fine dining with a great bottle of wine as well as a two-fisted sandwich at the bar in the blare of a ball game. It is a gathering place for influential politicians, sports and movie stars, and leaders of the business world; and it's where Joe and Jane Average kick back and relax after work. It is sophisticated, and it is loud and boisterous. Like its namesake, it defies classification. And like Harry, it is pure Chicago.

And the food—ah, the food! Here you will ease your knife into the juiciest, most flavorful prime steaks anywhere, steaks that earned Harry Caray's the award of Best Steakhouse in the city in a *Chicago Tribune* dining poll. To be considered the best steakhouse in Chicago is as good as it gets, for this is a city where great steaks are plentiful, and where savvy carnivores do not settle for second-best. When Executive Chef Garrick Dickie starts talking about beef— where to get the best, how to cook and serve it—you realize you are listening to a master. The plates that come from the kitchen at Harry Caray's restaurant define steak-house excellence. On the side of steaks you can get an awesome pound-plus baked potato that is long-cooked until its insides are creamy soft (or garlic mashed potatoes or Vesuvio

potatoes); and to drink, you can choose a bottle from 150 different wines from a cellar on which *Wine Spectator* has bestowed its Award of Excellence every year since 1989. Harry Caray's Restaurant serves large portions to reflect the larger-than-life personality of its namesake. And this cookbook offers large serving sizes to reflect the restaurant.

Beyond four-star steak and potatoes and a significant wine list, and beyond the elbow-bending pleasures of its spectacularly convivial barroom with the sixty-foot, six-inch long-bar (the distance from the pitcher's rubber to home plate), Harry Caray's also is an *Italian* steakhouse. Harry loved Italian food; and his friends remember that it was Italian that he ate nearly every night he went out (and he went out every night!); so he made his restaurant a place to come for linguine carbonara and fettuccine alfredo as good as any beyond the walls of Rome. In addition to its classic Italian meals, the menu boasts such uniquely Italian-American items as toasted ravioli (a salute to the neighborhood Italian cuisine of Harry Caray's original hometown, St. Louis) and Chicago's own chicken Vesuvio.

During the last few autumns, as an expression of the menu's Italian flair, Harry Caray's has held a Regional Italian Wine and Food Festival, during which the chefs supplement the regular fare with food specialties, cheeses, and wines from five regions of Italy for three days each. Last year, the featured regions were Piedmont, Tuscany, Veneto, Sardinia, and Emilia-Romagna; and among the local specialties offered on the celebration menus were Fontina and Parmigiano-Reggiano cheeses, white truffles, and Arborio rice from Piedmont. The

usual wine-by-the-glass list was replaced by a selection of forty-five Italian wines from fifteen different wineries in the featured regions. Each special dish was paired with a wine, and a wine flight was offered from a winery within the featured region of the day.

We sat in on a pre-shift meeting prior to lunch one day during the Italian festival when the chefs brought out the day's specialties for all the staff to taste and poured the day's wines for them to discuss. As we looked at the *Filetto di Manzo alla Pancetta* and sniffed the Masi-Campofiorni-Rosso del Veronese, we were taken by the care with which the food was prepared as well as by the diligent ritual of introducing the waitstaff to what was being served. This is NOT a restaurant where waiters learn simply to say, "Hello, my name is . . ." then recite a bunch of dishes about which they know little. The servers at Harry Caray's are trained extensively, dish by dish, meal by meal, wine by wine. They are tested—not only on their knowledge of the food and drink, but on what they know about the lore and history of the restaurant itself—and there are plenty of aspiring staff members who simply do not make the cut. Put another way: this restaurant is the culinary majors;

and a minor-league performance simply isn't good enough. Among those who do succeed and prove they know the most about Harry himself and the menu of the restaurant, the topmost winners are given a chance to throw out a pre-game ball at Wrigley Field.

If you said that Harry Caray's is the ultimate sports bar, you wouldn't be wrong; there's no better place in the world to watch a baseball game on one of the big TVs while knocking back beers and munching those addictive Holy Cow! potato chips for which Harry Caray's is famous. For a sports fan in general, a baseball fan in particular, or especially anyone who believes in the Chicago Cubs, this energetic establishment is home plate and home. Filled with artifacts that reflect the bigger-than-life passions of baseball's greatest announcer (and most outspoken fan), Harry

Caray's is like a big-time corporate hospitality box to which everyone's invited.

Aside from the extraordinary food and wine, aside from the Cubs connection, and even aside from the booming personality of Harry Caray himself, this restaurant is special because it is a vibrant expression of Chicago's heart and soul. The building itself, having achieved landmark status—a century-old industrial palazzo by the river—is imbued with city history and remains part of a vibrant downtown. Its capacious raw-brick-and-mahogany dining rooms and thick white tablecloths express a broad-shouldered generosity that defines Windy City dining. Few people come here to eat meager meals. There's plenty of room on these tables for plenty of food. And there is a forceful sense of hospitality in this place, whether at the bar or at a dining room table, that feels at once rich and democratic. Only in Chicago!

Harry Caray's is a crossroads. When a local TV or radio station needs to interview either a Chicago bigwig or someone who is "the voice of the people"—about any subject of public interest including, but not limited to, sports—it is common to bring the cameras and microphones into Harry Caray's place. "Whenever I take people out in Chicago and want to show them what the city is all about," former Illinois governor Jim Edgar once proclaimed, "I take them to Harry Caray's."

Harry Caray's Restaurant

33 West Kinzie Street

Chicago, IL 60610

(773) Holy–Cow

www.harrycarays.com

HARRY CARAY

1914–1998

More than an award-winning professional broadcaster, Harry Caray was the ultimate baseball fan. He relished being part of the major leagues, and his outspoken passion was so intense that at his Holy Name Cathedral funeral service in 1998 the pipe organ played "Take Me Out to the Ball Game." Now, every year sometime between his death date (February 18) and his birthday (March 1) Harry Caray's restaurant hosts a worldwide toast during which hundreds of thousands of people from fifty states and some fifty countries all raise a glass (preferably of Budweiser, Harry's brand) and say, "Here's to Harry."

He was as famous as any player, and he became as much a symbol of the Cubs as Wrigley Field itself. He was a people's hero who felt that his primary duty as an announcer was to be the voice of the people in the bleachers. (When he was with the White Sox at Comiskey Park on the South Side of Chicago, he occasionally broadcast games directly from the bleachers!)

"His whole life was devoted to baseball," recalls Grant DePorter, managing partner of the restaurant. "Baseball and going into restaurants and bars." Grant noted that he was such a gregarious man that *his* table at Harry Caray's was always the one closest to the bar, where the action was. He liked to be in the middle of everything.

Chicago Tribune food critic Phil Vettel wrote of one visit when he was seated next to Harry's table. "I was amazed at his cheerful willingness to set down his fork and exchange pleasantries with everyone who stopped by (and that night, everyone did), treating each banality ('The Cubs gotta get some pitching, Harry!') as fresh insight while his dinner grew colder." Harry signed autographs all the time. He loved to remind critics of his outspoken ways, that it was the fans he felt he answered to, not the bosses. He would talk baseball with anyone who had an opinion; and his phone number was listed in the phone book.

He once declared himself the most listened-to Italian-American singer in the world because even though he couldn't carry a tune, he led thousands of fans in a rendition of "Take Me Out to the Ball Game" during every seventh-inning stretch of every home game he broadcast. His exclamation, "HOLY COW!" when someone hit a homer became the best-known sports-broadcasting catchphrase of all time. Now most vividly recalled for his last gig as the voice of the Chicago Cubs, Harry spent fifty-three years in

the broadcast booth, first gaining fame in his original hometown of St. Louis, where he began announcing Cards games in 1945. A quarter of a century later, he moved to the Oakland A's for a season, then to Chicago as the TV/radio voice of the Chicago White Sox for a decade. In 1982 he came to Wrigley Field.

Perhaps the only thing Harry Caray liked as much as baseball was the night life: wining and dining. He once estimated that during his lifetime he had drunk 300,000 alcoholic drinks, 73,000 of which were Budweisers. "Harry lived to go out with friends," recalls his widow, Dutchie. "Having been with both the American and National leagues, he went everywhere,

Harry's table was typically occupied until 3:00 A.M.

and he knew the good places to eat and drink in every city. He'd start with three or four martinis—Bombay gin with anchovy olives—then he *dined*. When Harry went into a restaurant, that table was gone for the night. He didn't leave until after midnight. He was tireless. He would stay out until 3:00 A.M."

The man who was dubbed "Mayor of Rush Street" in the 1970s when he was with the White Sox was especially fond of Italian food. Born Harry Christopher Carabina, of French-Romanian and Italian descent, Harry made a point of finding the great Italian restaurants in every city he visited. He especially loved pasta with marinara sauce, shrimp with garlic, and Chicago's own chicken Vesuvio.

For all he loved to eat, he couldn't cook a thing. Dutchie remembers, "He could not pour coffee. If he tried, most of it wound up on the floor. He once called me to ask how to cut a grapefruit; and there was the time when I was with my family for Christmas. He called to find out where the garbage bags were. I told him, but he called back a few minutes later and said, 'I found them, but the ones I found had only one side.'" Dutchie grins and says she refrained from advising him to get some duct tape and start putting the one-sided bags together.

When the restaurant that bears his name opened in 1987, it wasn't just a business venture. It was an expression of Harry Caray's twin passions for baseball and food. "I've wanted a place like this for a long time," he wrote. "A place where I could hang out, relax, and talk sports with my friends. . . . You know, after all those years on the road dining out, I acquired a taste for really good food. . . . Prime steaks, classic Italian, good drink, and a whole lot more."

Steve Stone, whose fifteen years in the broadcast booth as color commentator alongside Harry resulted in the high-spirited memoir *Where's Harry?*, is a fount of stories that show just how popular Harry was, especially in his hometown. One time, a transit bus stopped in front of a Chicago hotel just as Harry was about to walk in the door. The riders in the bus saw him and, Stone writes, "went nuts. People wouldn't sit down and the bus driver couldn't move with all of the hysteria." To help ease the situation, Harry climbed aboard the bus and shook the hand—or high-fived—each and every passenger, then exited the back door. Stone recalls, "As the bus pulled away, the happy fans serenaded him with 'Take Me Out to the Ball Game.'

"How many other broadcasters in the history of the world would draw that kind of response?"

· SOUPS ·

Minestrone Soup

Tuscan Bean and Sausage Soup

Italian Onion Soup

Creamy Roasted Garlic Soup

Cream of Zucchini Soup

Tomato Basil Soup

Potato and Onion Soup

Creamy Potato and Pancetta Soup

Minestrone Soup

Everything served at Harry Caray's is generously apportioned—a style especially appropriate for minestrone, which means "big soup". While canned broth can be used, homemade chicken stock makes it sing.

3 tablespoons olive oil	½ cup diced green beans
6 ounces prosciutto, sliced thick	¾ cup kidney beans
½ cup diced carrots	¾ cup garbanzo beans
½ cup diced celery	2 cups cannellini beans
½ cup diced onions	1 cup green peas
½ cup sliced cabbage, optional	Salt and pepper
½ cup tomato purée (4-ounce can)	½ cup cooked spinach
8 cups homemade chicken stock (see page 94), or equivalent amount canned low-sodium chicken broth	½ cup cooked escarole
½ cup diced zucchini	½ cup cooked tubetti pasta
½ cup peeled diced potatoes, cooked al dente	

Heat the olive oil in a large stockpot over medium heat. Add the prosciutto and sauté for 4 to 5 minutes. Add the carrots, celery, onions, potatoes, and cabbage, if using, and sauté the mixture until the vegetables become translucent. Stir in the tomato purée and slowly add the chicken stock and bring to a boil. Add the zucchini, potatoes, green beans, kidney beans, garbanzo beans, cannellini beans, green peas, and salt and pepper to taste. Simmer over low heat until the mixture is warmed through, about 15 minutes. Immediately prior to serving, add the spinach, escarole, and tubetti.

MAKES 6 SERVINGS

Tuscan Bean and Sausage Soup

Also known as white Italian kidney beans, cannellini are a variety of haricots. Their silky smooth texture pairs well with rugged sausage.

1	head escarole, cored
2	teaspoons olive oil
¾	pound Italian sausage
½	cup chopped Spanish onion
½	cup chopped carrots
1	tablespoon minced garlic
3	tablespoons water
1	tablespoon olive oil
2	teaspoons dry thyme
1	bay leaf
2	(15-ounce) cans cannellini beans, drained and rinsed
2	cups homemade chicken stock (see page 94), or equivalent amount canned low-sodium chicken broth
	Salt and black pepper

Blanch the escarole by placing it in boiling water for 1 minute and then rinsing it in cold water. Preheat the oven to 350°F. Heat the olive oil in a sauté pan over medium heat. Add the sausage and brown on both sides. Transfer the sausage to a sheet pan and bake the sausage in the oven for approximately 12 to 15 minutes or until cooked through. Drain the excess oil off the sausage, allow it to cool, and then chop into bite-size pieces. In a medium stockpot, combine the onion, carrots, garlic, water, and olive oil. Simmer the mixture over medium heat until the onions are clear. Stir in the thyme, bay leaf, cannellini beans, and chicken stock. Bring the mixture to a boil, and then reduce the heat and simmer for 15 to 20 minutes. Take half of the mixture and purée it in a food processor or blender. Return the puréed mixture to the stockpot. Stir in the sausage and escarole. Add the salt and pepper to taste. Simmer for an additional 5 minutes and serve.

MAKES 6 TO 8 SERVINGS

Italian Onion Soup

We all know French onion soup. Here's the Italian version, made with Chicago's stout Italian bread and powerful grated Asiago cheese—a sharper, more flavorful version of Parmesan.

---

2   tablespoons unsalted butter

2   tablespoons olive oil

5   medium sweet onions (Vidalia if available), sliced

2   teaspoons flour

¾   cup Marsala wine

¼   cup dry sherry

4   cups homemade beef stock (see page 95),
    or equivalent amount of canned low-sodium beef broth

    Salt

    Black pepper

4   to 6 (¾-inch) slices stale Italian bread

¾   cup shredded Asiago cheese

Heat the butter and olive oil in a medium stockpot over medium heat. Sauté the onions, stirring frequently until they become soft. Add the flour and stir well. Add the Marsala and sherry and simmer until the wine reduces by half. Add the beef stock and simmer for 20 more minutes. Season with the salt and black pepper to taste. Ladle the soup into individual bowls. Top each bowl of soup with a slice of the bread and sprinkle with Asiago cheese.

MAKES 4 TO 6 SERVINGS

Creamy Roasted Garlic Soup

When roasted, even ferocious garlic develops a pussycat personality. With potatoes and cream, six whole bulbs here become the foundation of a mellow soup.

6	bulbs garlic
¼	cup olive oil
1	Spanish onion, chopped
⅓	cup Marsala wine
4	cups homemade chicken stock (see page 94), or equivalent amount canned low-sodium chicken broth
1	large russet potato, peeled and diced
1	cup heavy whipping cream
	Salt
	Black pepper
¼	cup chopped chives

Preheat the oven to 400°F. Remove the top quarter inch of each garlic bulb. Place the bulbs in a baking dish and drizzle with the olive oil. Bake for 1 hour or until the garlic is soft. Remove the garlic bulbs from the oven and allow them to cool. Squeeze the garlic out of the bulbs and reserve the olive oil from the baking dish. Heat the reserved oil in a large stockpot and sauté the onion until clear. Add the Marsala wine and reduce by one-third then add the chicken stock and bring the mixture to a boil. Add the potato and roasted garlic and reduce the heat to a simmer for approximately ½ hour or until the potato is soft. Purée the soup in a blender or food processor and return the soup to the pot. Add the cream ¼ cup at a time, stirring slowly. Season with the salt and pepper to taste. Simmer until the soup thickens. Garnish the soup with the chives.

MAKES 4 TO 6 SERVINGS

Cream of Zucchini Soup

Zucchini is on menus throughout Italy, especially in the South. When we visited Rome, we had memorable pizza topped with little matchstick pieces of the ubiquitous vegetable. Here it is in a creamy-sweet soup.

3	tablespoons butter
1	pound zucchini, diced
1	clove garlic, finely chopped
¾	cup finely chopped Spanish onions
3¼	cups homemade chicken stock (see page 94), or equivalent amount canned low-sodium chicken broth
1	sprig fresh thyme
1	leaf fresh sage
	Salt and black pepper
¾	cup cream
1	tablespoon chopped green onions

In a large stockpot, melt the butter over medium heat. Add the zucchini, garlic, and Spanish onions and sauté until the onions become clear. Add the chicken stock, thyme, sage, and salt and black pepper to taste and simmer covered for 15 minutes. Remove the thyme and sage. Purée the soup in a blender or food processor and return it to the stockpot. Stir in the cream ¼ cup at a time, stirring slowly, and simmer for 10 more minutes. Serve in bowls and garnish with the green onions.

MAKES 4 SERVINGS

Tomato Basil Soup

T omato and basil: from soup to sorbet (yes, sorbet!), these are the most-paired ingredients in the Italian kitchen. Onions and carrots add a deep vegetable sweetness.

---

2   tablespoons olive oil

⅓   cup diced onions

⅓   cup diced carrots

1   bay leaf

1   (32-ounce) can whole plum tomatoes, and juice

2   cups homemade chicken stock (see page 94),
    or equivalent amount canned low-sodium chicken broth

    Dash of Tabasco

    Dash of Worcestershire sauce

1   tablespoon granulated garlic

    Salt and white pepper

¼   cup julianned basil

In a medium stockpot, heat the olive oil over a medium flame. Sauté the onions and carrots until the onions are translucent. Add the bay leaf and tomatoes. Simmer the mixture for 15 minutes. Remove the bay leaf and add the chicken stock, Tabasco, and Worcestershire. Simmer the mixture for an additional 15 minutes. Purée the mixture in a blender or food processor. Return the mixture to the heat and season with the garlic and salt and pepper to taste. Add the basil and simmer for 10 more minutes. Serve with crusty Italian bread or crackers.

MAKES 6 SERVINGS

Potato and Onion Soup

Cooking potatoes in beef stock gives the starchy vegetable a robust flavor that all meat lovers will appreciate. A sprinkle of Parmesan on each serving adds just the right zip.

1½ tablespoons butter

1½ tablespoons extra virgin olive oil

1½ cups peeled and sliced Spanish onions

4½ cups homemade beef stock (see page 95)
     or equivalent amount of canned, low-sodium beef broth

3   cups peeled and diced potatoes

     Salt and white pepper

3   tablespoons grated Parmesan cheese

Melt the butter over medium heat in a large sauté pan and add the olive oil. Add the onions and sauté until they become translucent and turn a light brown. In a large stockpot, bring the beef stock to a boil. Reduce the heat and add the potatoes. Simmer over medium heat until the potatoes are soft, about 20 minutes. Add the onions to the stockpot and simmer for an additional 15 minutes. Salt and pepper the soup to taste. Sprinkle the Parmesan cheese on top and serve.

MAKES 4 TO 6 SERVINGS

Creamy Potato and Pancetta Soup

To say that pancetta is Italian bacon doesn't do it justice. The sweet cured pork is amended with a hail of black pepper and plenty of garlic to attain maximum potency. It tastes perfect when paired with gentle-flavored foods, such as potatoes and cream.

---

4   large russet potatoes, peeled

½   pound pancetta, thinly sliced and diced

3   shallots, chopped

3   cups homemade chicken stock (see page 94),
    or equivalent amount canned low-sodium chicken broth

3   cups heavy cream
    Salt and white pepper

½   cup sour cream

1   tablespoon chopped chives

Boil the potatoes until soft. Drain off the water and set the potatoes aside. In a large stockpot over medium heat, sauté the pancetta until it becomes crispy. Pour off half the fat, add the shallots, and sauté until they become translucent. Whisk in the chicken stock and heavy cream. Bring the mixture to a slow boil and add the potatoes. Bring the mixture to a full boil. Purée the mixture with a hand mixer. If the soup is too thick, add more chicken stock. Add salt and white pepper to taste. Garnish the soup with a dollop of the sour cream and the chives.

MAKES 6 TO 8 SERVINGS

33 WEST KINZIE

West Kinzie Street in Chicago's River North is an easy walk from the city's grand hotels and swank shops. As you gaze upon the imposing edifice that is Number 33, you are looking at a piece of Chicago's soul—a century-old brick building that, while smaller than the modern high-rise concrete and glass all around it, seems huge.

Number 33 appears to be a whole city block. In a town that bristles with awesome structural design, this place has personality beyond architecture. In fact, it was designated a historic landmark in Chicago in 2001. Designed as the Chicago Varnish Company Building by Henry Ives Cobb in 1895, its stepped-gable tile roof and brick-and-limestone façade make it one of the Midwest's most perfect examples of Dutch Renaissance Revival style. The varnish company wanted a building by the river for easy transportation of its product. At the time, the now-stylish part of town called River North was known as The Sands, an area where gambling, prostitution, and vice flourished.

In the 1930s, gangster Al Capone's henchman Frank "the Enforcer" Nitti was said to have used a fourth-floor apartment in the building as a lookout while his in-laws, the Caravetta family, packaged and distributed Italian cheeses down below. After several years of ambiguous use and ownership, it was purchased in 1971 by the Canteen Corporation, which turned it into

(L to R) Grant DePorter, Marv Levy, Dutchie Caray, Ryne Sandberg, and director of marketing Beth Goldberg Heller

the Kinzie Street Steak and Chop House; and in 1986 after a full restoration, the building was leased to Harry Caray and friends as the home of his namesake restaurant. But as a lessee, Harry Caray's Italian Steakhouse was vulnerable to a landlord's whims; and after Harry's death, when rumors surfaced that a New York company was going to buy it for who-knows-what, Harry's heirs decided to do something. In October 2002, a small group of investors, including his widow, Dutchie Caray, former Cubs second baseman Ryne Sandberg, sportscaster Bob Costas, and Buffalo Bills coach Marv Levy, bought the building. Grant DePorter, managing partner, said his group felt they had to make the purchase to ensure the longtime

survival of the steakhouse Harry Caray started. "This is a restaurant that will last 100 years," DePorter said.

That sense of destiny radiates from 33 West Kinzie, inside and out. Aside from its impressive design, the building's punch is also delivered by a huge banner that says simply, "HOLY COW" book-ended by caricatures of Harry, who made that expression his catchphrase.

The inside is a luxury of materials that create posh ambience: rich mahogany paneling and thick white tablecloths are aligned in precision among raw brick walls. The scale of the place is imposing. The downstairs dining rooms are voluminous, with lots of tables and vast amounts of elbow room. The barroom features a bar that is sixty feet-six inches-long—the exact distance from the pitcher's rubber to home plate. ("NOT the distance from the mound to home plate," the bartender made a point of telling us one conversational afternoon.) The room contains twelve televisions, including a 120-inch big screen on which a "sing along with Harry" is featured at 7:30 every night: tribute to his unfailing rendition of "Take Me Out to the Ball Game" during the seventh-inning

stretch of each home game he announced. Upstairs, banquet rooms can accommodate groups of up to four hundred people. The Old Comiskey Room houses a grand antique bar originally from Arlington Park Racetrack along with a mural of the original Comiskey Park. The Wrigley Room boasts a wall-size mural of Wrigley Field and the Chicago skyline.

Even the sidewalk outside the restaurant's front door is something special. It is set with a series of granite slabs with a gold Harry face caricature that serve as tributes to Harry himself, as well as to the men who were most important to him in his career. This is known as Harry Caray's Walk of Fame.

• SALADS •

Chopped Salad with Chicken

Caesar Salad

Chicken Vesuvio Salad

Pesto Chicken Pasta Salad

Antipasto Salad

Mixed Greens Salad

Tuscan Salad

Panzanella (Tuscan Bread Salad)

Great Tomato, Onion, and Anchovy Salad

Dutchie's Salad

Broccoli Salad

Chilled Lobster Salad with Garlic Toast Points

Rotini Pasta Salad

Chopped Salad with Chicken

While this recipe calls for mixed green lettuces, it also requires iceberg. As a textural counterpoint to velvet-soft diced chicken, only iceberg has the necessary crunch. With pancetta, Gorgonzola cheese, and avocado in addition to the chicken itself, it is, definitely a meal rather than an accompaniment.

1   large head iceberg lettuce, chopped

8   ounces mixed green lettuces (we use green leaf lettuce, romaine, radicchio, and mesclun greens)

¾   cup crumbled Gorgonzola cheese, halved

¾   cup thinly sliced and diced cooked pancetta (Italian bacon), halved

¾   cup diced avocado, halved

¾   cup diced tomato, halved

¾   cup sliced scallions, halved

3   (7-ounce) grilled chicken breasts, diced

1½   cups sweet herb vinaigrette (see page 97)

Mix together the iceberg lettuce, mixed greens, half of the Gorgonzola, half of the pancetta, half of the avocado, half of the tomato, half of the scallions, and the chicken breasts. Toss with the vinaigrette. Arrange the salad on individual plates, and sprinkle the remaining Gorgonzola, pancetta, avocado, tomato, and scallions on top of the salads.

MAKES 6 TO 8 SERVINGS

Caesar Salad

The reason many restaurants make Caesar salad at the table is that it never should be mixed in advance. If not served immediately, Caesar salad can get watery and its romaine leaves limp.

FOR THE GARLIC CROUTONS:

2   cups cubed, crust-off French or Italian bread

1   tablespoon grated Parmesan cheese

1   teaspoon granulated garlic

    Pinch of salt

    Pinch of white pepper

    Pinch of paprika

    Pinch of oregano

¼   cup melted butter

FOR THE SALAD:

1½ pounds cleaned and chopped hearts of romaine

1   cup Harry's Caesar dressing (see page 99)

⅓   cup grated Parmesan cheese

½   cup shaved Parmigiano-Reggiano cheese

To make the garlic croutons, preheat the oven to 350°F. In a small bowl, combine the cubed bread, Parmesan cheese, garlic, salt, white pepper, paprika, and oregano. Place the melted butter in a medium bowl and toss the seasoned bread cubes in the butter. Spread the bread cubes on a cookie sheet and bake in the oven for 10 to 15 minutes or until they become crunchy and golden brown.

To assemble the salad, toss the hearts of romaine and Caesar dressing in a large salad bowl. Top with the croutons, Parmesan cheese, and shaved Parmigiano-Reggiano. Serve immediately. To make this into an entrée salad, add grilled chicken, grilled shrimp, or grilled sirloin.

MAKES 4 SERVINGS

Chicken Vesuvio Salad

While conventional chicken Vesuvio is a hot entrée, Harry Caray's has made it into a salad. Nearly all of its ingredients—plus lettuce—are arranged on a plate and dressed with vinaigrette. The basic culinary principle at work is that if something can fit on a plate, Harry Caray's can probably make it Vesuvio style.

½   cup frozen peas

2   large Idaho russet potatoes

⅓   cup olive oil

4   (7-ounce) skinless, boneless chicken breasts

6   cloves whole garlic

½   teaspoon salt

½   teaspoon pepper

1   teaspoon oregano

1   teaspoon granulated garlic

1   tablespoon chopped parsley

¾   cup white wine

¾   cup homemade chicken stock (page 94), or equivalent amount canned low-sodium chicken broth

1½   pounds mixed salad greens (we use iceberg, green leaf lettuce, romaine, radicchio, and mesclun greens)

1   cup Italian vinaigrette (see page 100)

Preheat the oven to 375°F. To blanch the peas, place in boiling water for 1 minute, then rinse them in cold water to stop the cooking. Peel the potatoes and cut into quarters lengthwise. In a large roasting pan, heat the olive oil over medium heat. Add the potatoes and sauté them until golden brown, turning repeatedly, approximately 8 minutes. Add the chicken and whole garlic to the pan with the potatoes and sauté lightly on both sides until golden brown. Season the potatoes and chicken with the salt, pepper, oregano, granulated garlic, and parsley. Remove the garlic cloves and discard. Deglaze the pan with the wine. Add the chicken stock and immediately remove the roasting pan from the stove and put it into the oven for 15 to 20 minutes or until the chicken reaches an internal temperature of 155°F. Dice the potatoes and cut the chicken breasts into strips. To serve, toss the mixed greens with the Italian vinaigrette and mound the mixed greens in the center of four individual plates. Place the sliced chicken breasts on top of the lettuce and sprinkle the potatoes and the peas around the chicken.

MAKES 4 ENTRÉE SALADS

Pesto Chicken Pasta Salad

This lively salad is great as a meal unto itself, and especially welcome at a covered dish dinner.

---

3   (7-ounce) skinless, boneless chicken breasts
    Lawry's seasoned salt
    Black pepper
1½ pounds tri-color fusilli, cooked al dente
1   red pepper, seeded and julienned
1   green pepper, seeded and julienned
1   yellow pepper, seeded and julienned
¾   cup pesto sauce (see page 85)
¼   cup diced hearts of palm
½   cup quartered artichoke hearts
12 kalamata olives, pitted and halved

Season the chicken breasts well with the seasoned salt and black pepper. Grill or broil the chicken until it is cooked to an internal temperature of 155°F. Dice the chicken into bite-size pieces and chill. In a large mixing bowl, toss the diced chicken, pasta, peppers, and pesto sauce together. Mound the pasta mixture in the center of a large serving platter. Arrange the hearts of palm and the artichoke hearts around the outside of the platter. Garnish the top with the olives.

MAKES 4 TO 6 SALADS

Antipasto Salad

Chicago likes big salads, especially big salads that have lots of ingredients not normally found in a typical bowl of greens. This one includes virtually all the meats and even cheese from an antipasto platter, plus greens. Make sure all the ingredients are diced very fine. Your goal should be to have a wondrous bit of nearly everything on each forkful.

½ cup green beans

1½ pounds mixed salad greens (we use iceberg, green leaf lettuce, romaine, radicchio, and mesclun greens)

½ cup tri-color diced peppers

⅓ cup thinly sliced and diced provolone cheese

⅓ cup thinly sliced and diced soppressata

⅓ cup thinly sliced and diced Genoa salami

⅓ cup thinly sliced and diced cured coppa

⅓ cup thinly sliced and diced mortadella

⅓ cup quartered artichoke hearts

⅓ cup diced hearts of palm

1 cup Italian vinaigrette (see page 100)

12 kalamata olives

Blanch the green beans by placing them in boiling water for 1 minute and then rinsing them in cold water. In a large mixing bowl, toss together the salad greens, tri-color peppers, and blanched green beans. In a medium mixing bowl, combine the provolone, soppressata, salami, coppa, and mortadella. On six individual plates, mound the lettuce mixture in the middle. Top each salad with one-sixth of the meat and cheese mixture. Arrange the artichoke hearts and hearts of palm around the edge of each plate. Drizzle each salad with the Italian vinaigrette. Garnish each plate with 2 kalamata olives. Serve immediately.

MAKES 6 SALADS

Mixed Greens Salad

The salad itself is good, but what makes it especially delicious are the freshly made croutons and the crunchy green beans.

FOR THE GARLIC CROUTONS:

2   cups cubed, crust-off French or Italian bread
1   tablespoon grated Parmesan cheese
1   teaspoon granulated garlic
     Pinch of salt
     Pinch of white pepper
     Pinch of paprika
     Pinch of oregano
¼   cup melted butter

FOR THE SALAD:

⅔   cup green beans
1½   pounds mixed salad greens (we use iceberg,
        green leaf lettuce, romaine, radicchio, and mesclun greens)
⅔   cup tri-color julienned peppers
     Dressing of choice

To make the garlic croutons, preheat the oven to 350°F. Combine the cubed bread, Parmesan cheese, garlic, salt, white pepper, paprika, and oregano in a small bowl. Place the melted butter in a medium bowl and toss the seasoned bread in the butter. Spread the bread cubes out onto a cookie sheet and bake in the oven for 10 to 15 minutes or until the cubes become golden brown. Blanch the green beans by placing them in boiling water for 1 minute and then rinsing them with cold water.

To make the salad, blanch the green beans by placing them in boiling water for 1 minute and then rinsing them with cold water. In a large mixing bowl, toss together the blanched green beans, mixed greens, and peppers. Mound the greens mixture in the center of six individual salad plates. Sprinkle with the garlic croutons and drizzle with the dressing. Serve immediately.

MAKES 6 SALADS

Tuscan Salad

A zesty salad with plenty of substance but no meat: good for vegetarians, but not vegans because it demands the luxury of fresh mozzarella—the best fresh mozzarella you can find.

1½ pounds mixed salad greens (we use iceberg, green leaf lettuce, romaine, radicchio, and mesclun greens)

1 red onion, thinly sliced

⅔ cup garbanzo beans

⅔ cup sliced cucumbers

⅔ cup diced beefsteak tomatoes

1¼ pounds fresh mozzarella cheese, sliced ¼ inch thick

⅔ cup sliced hearts of palm

1 cup Italian vinaigrette (see page 100)

12 kalamata olives

12 pepperoncini

1 roasted red pepper, julienned

In a large mixing bowl, toss together the salad greens, onion, garbanzo beans, cucumbers, tomatoes, cheese, hearts of palm, and vinaigrette. Mound the salad mixture in the center of six individual plates. Garnish each plate with 2 kalamata olives and 2 pepperoncini. Top each salad with a few of the roasted red pepper pieces. Serve immediately.

MAKES 6 SALADS

Panzanella (Tuscan Bread Salad)

If you're the type who can never get enough croutons on your salad, this is a good one to keep in mind. A flavorful panzanella salad is a summer standard in many Italian *trattorias* (restaurants).

FOR THE DRESSING:

3	tablespoons red wine vinegar
6	tablespoons olive oil
1	tablespoon chopped parsley
	Salt
	Black pepper

FOR THE SALAD:

1	loaf stale Italian white bread
4	tablespoons olive oil
3	scallions, sliced into rings
1	garlic clove, finely chopped
1	cup peeled, seeded, and diced tomatoes
1	cup diced cucumbers
2	yellow bell peppers, cored, seeded, and cut into ¼-inch-thick rings
2	heads frisée lettuce, stemmed and cleaned
8	anchovy fillets
2	teaspoons capers

To make the dressing, whisk together the vinegar, olive oil, parsley, and salt and black pepper to taste.

To make the salad, cut the Italian loaf into ¾-inch cubes. In a medium sauté pan, heat the olive oil over medium heat. Sauté the bread cubes on all sides until golden brown. Drain the bread on paper towels. In a large salad bowl, toss together the bread cubes, scallions, garlic, tomatoes, cucumbers, and pepper rings. Toss the salad with the dressing. Let it rest 5 to 10 minutes before serving.

To serve, make a bed on each plate with several pieces of the frisée. Mound the salad on top of the frisée and top each salad with anchovies and capers.

MAKES 6 SERVINGS

THE HARRY CARAY'S RESTAURANT COOKBOOK

Great Tomato, Onion, and Anchovy Salad

Here is a simple dish of few ingredients, each of which must be excellent. If you can't get fresh, flavorful tomatoes and sweet onions, don't even bother.

---

9   *on-the-vine tomatoes*

1   *large sweet onion (Vidalia if available)*

¾   *cup Italian vinaigrette (see page 100)*

6   *large leaves of romaine lettuce*

12 *anchovy fillets*

Cut the tomatoes into large wedges. Peel and thinly slice the onion. In a large mixing bowl, toss the tomatoes, onions, and Italian vinaigrette until well combined. On a large serving platter, make a bed using the romaine leaves. Pile the tomato and onion mixture on top of the Romaine and garnish with the anchovies.

MAKES 6 SERVINGS

Dutchie's Salad

When we asked her why this salad bore her name, Dutchie Caray told us that it's made of everything she likes. Its tender greens are combined with a kaleidoscopic combination of ingredients: tart apples, sweet pears, crunchy walnuts, and heady Gorgonzola cheese all mixed with fruit-flavored vinaigrette. With a few pieces of grilled chicken, this is one fine meal!

FOR THE CANDIED WALNUTS:

1   tablespoon butter

1   cup walnuts

¼   cup brown sugar

1   tablespoon molasses

FOR THE SALAD:

1   pound mesclun greens

2   Granny Smith apples, cored and sliced

2   D'Anjou or Bartlett pears, cored and sliced

1   cup crumbled Gorgonzola cheese

¾   cup raspberry vinaigrette (see page 98)

To candy-glaze the walnuts, preheat the oven to 350°F. Melt the butter in a sauté pan over medium heat. Stir in the walnuts, brown sugar, and molasses until the walnuts are thoroughly coated. Spread the sugar-coated walnuts on a cookie sheet. Bake in the oven for 10 minutes. Set aside to cool.

To make the salad, mound the mesclun greens in the center of six individual plates. Alternate sliced apples and sliced pears around the greens. Top the greens with the candied walnuts and the Gorgonzola cheese. Drizzle with raspberry vinaigrette. Serve immediately.

MAKES 6 SERVINGS

DUTCHIE

How fitting! Harry Caray met his wife Dutchie in a restaurant. It was 1969; Harry had been married twice but was single for the third and last time when he walked into Brennan's outside St. Louis after broadcasting a Cardinals game. There he spotted a woman he wanted to know better. She was Dolores Goldmann, having dinner with friends. Known as Dutchie for her ethnic background, she had little interest in dating anyone, let alone getting married. "I was divorced and trying to raise five kids," she recalls. "I didn't have a hell of a lot of time to do anything else other than cook, clean, iron, wash, and get the kids ready for school."

But Harry was a determined man. The next few times Dutchie went to Brennan's, Harry just happened to be there. For six years he pursued her, phoning from cities all around the country as he traveled to broadcast games. Finally she said yes to his entreaties; and on May 19, 1975, they were married by a justice of the peace at Chicago's Ambassador East hotel. After the ceremony they went straight to Comiskey Park, where Harry broadcast a White Sox game with his new bride by his side.

Dutchie was with Harry until he passed away in 1998; and although she didn't always go on the road with him, their closeness strengthened and Harry became what she remembers as her best friend. "He was fun to be around," Dutchie says. "Harry never had any down days. He just enjoyed life—every minute of it—he lived it to the fullest."

Since Harry's death, Dutchie has remained involved in his favorite charity, the Maryville Youth Academy, and in the restaurant, where she often dines at what used to be his table in the corner. Today she is especially grateful that Harry put his foot down when she went on spring cleaning campaigns and wanted to dispose of the boxes of memorabilia, photographs, and clippings that Harry kept throughout his life; now, they form the nucleus of the décor at the restaurant.

Broccoli Salad

A great dish for broccoli lovers, for here the florets retain their snap and flavor as they are highlighted by a bath of oil, garlic, and lemon juice. The peppers and kalamata olives make it a beauty.

4	cups broccoli florets
½	cup olive oil
2	tablespoons chopped garlic
	Juice of 2 lemons
	Salt and white pepper
½	red pepper, seeded and julienned
4	kalamata olives

Blanch the broccoli by placing it in boiling water for 3 to 4 minutes and then rinsing it with cold water to stop the cooking. In a medium mixing bowl, combine the blanched broccoli, olive oil, garlic, and lemon juice. Season the mixture with salt and white pepper to taste. Transfer the mixture to a salad bowl, top with the red pepper, and garnish with the olives.

MAKES 4 SERVINGS

Chilled Lobster Salad with Garlic Toast Points

Meat from rock lobster tails is essential. It has a brawny texture that holds its own with the rest of these vivid ingredients.

FOR THE GARLIC TOAST:

½	stick butter, softened
2	cloves garlic, finely chopped
	Pinch of salt
	Pinch of white pepper
	Pinch of paprika
1	loaf crusty Italian bread, sliced into ¾-inch slices
1	tablespoon freshly grated Parmigiano-Reggiano cheese

FOR THE SALAD:

3	pounds cold-water lobster tails
1	pound Roma tomatoes, diced
1	large red onion, thinly sliced
4	tablespoons red wine vinegar
½	cup extra virgin olive oil
2	cloves garlic, finely chopped
¼	teaspoon crushed red pepper flakes
4	to 6 large pieces green leaf lettuce
	Kosher salt
	Cracked black pepper

Preheat the oven to 350°F. To make the garlic toast, in a small mixing bowl combine the butter, garlic, salt, white pepper, and paprika. Brush the garlic mixture on the bread slices. Sprinkle each slice with the Parmigiano-Reggiano cheese. Bake the bread slices on a cookie sheet until they are crispy and brown, 5 to 10 minutes.

To make the salad, bring enough water to cover the lobster tails to a boil over high heat in a large stockpot. Place the lobster tails in the water and boil until the shells become pink. Chill the cooked lobster tails, remove the shell, and dice the meat into cubes. In a large mixing bowl, toss the lobster meat, tomatoes, onion, vinegar, olive oil, garlic, and red pepper flakes. Add the kosher salt and cracked black pepper to taste. Place a piece of the green leaf lettuce on each plate. Mound the lobster salad on the top of the lettuce. Garnish each plate with several slices of the garlic toast.

MAKES 4 TO 6 SERVINGS

Rotini Pasta Salad

Rotini is a short spiral-shaped pasta that works well with this intensely flavored and brightly colored dish.

1	pound rotini pasta, cooked al dente
1/3	cup olive oil
3	tablespoons balsamic vinegar
1	tablespoon chopped garlic
1	tablespoon chopped fresh basil
1/2	teaspoon oregano
1/2	teaspoon salt
1/4	teaspoon black pepper
1/3	cup chopped celery
1/4	cup chopped red onion
1/2	cup diced tri-color peppers
1/4	cup chopped carrots

In a large bowl, toss the rotini with the olive oil, balsamic vinegar, garlic, basil, oregano, salt, black pepper, celery, onion, peppers, and carrots. Chill and serve.

MAKES 6 TO 8 SERVINGS

· SANDWICHES ·

Italian Beef Sandwiches Au Jus

Chicken Parmigiana Sandwiches

Grilled Yellowfin Tuna (Ahi) Sandwiches

Roasted Turkey Club Sandwiches

Chicken Vesuvio Sandwiches

Grilled New York Strip Sirloin Sandwiches

Pepper-Crusted Beef Medallion Sandwiches

Italian Meatball Sandwiches

Italian Beef Sandwiches Au Jus

While many people know of Harry Caray's as a fine, sit-down dinner restaurant, it is also a place that attracts hoards of Chicagoans who come to Harry's barroom to have a quick lunch off the sandwich cart. From 11:30 A.M. to 4:00 P.M. every day (Sundays from 12 to 4), roast beef, prime rib, and turkey are carved to order. The beef is made and served the distinctive Chicago way known as "Italian beef." Another local specialty with Italian character but no actual heritage in the old country, Italian beef is a citywide passion, always served *au jus* with peppers on a length of crusty Italian bread.

1 plus 1 tablespoon olive oil	Salt
1 carrot, sliced	½ green bell pepper, seeded and sliced into 4 pieces
2 celery ribs, sliced	½ yellow bell pepper, seeded and sliced into 4 pieces
1 yellow onion, chopped	
1 tablespoon chopped garlic	½ red bell pepper, seeded and sliced into 4 pieces
1 bay leaf	
½ teaspoon oregano	1 long loaf French bread, cut into 4 pieces
½ teaspoon basil	
½ teaspoon black pepper	1½ pounds thinly sliced roast beef
4 cups water	8 (1½-ounce) slices smoked mozzarella cheese
4 beef bouillon cubes	

In a medium saucepan heat 1 tablespoon of olive oil over medium heat. Add the carrot, celery, onion, garlic, bay leaf, oregano, basil, and pepper. Sauté until the onion turns translucent. Add the water and boullion cubes and simmer until the liquid reduces by half. Add salt to taste. Strain the *jus* mixture and return it to the saucepan. Preheat the oven to 350°F. In a sauté pan, heat the remaining olive oil to medium. Sauté the peppers until they are soft. Slice the French bread lengthwise. Stir the sliced roast beef in the *jus* for 30 seconds. Fill each French-bread piece with the *jus*-soaked roast beef. Top each sandwich with 1 slice each of the green, yellow, and red bell peppers. Cover each sandwich with 2 slices of smoked mozzarella and bake the sandwiches in the oven for 5 minutes or until the cheese is melted. Serve with a side of *jus*.

MAKES 4 SANDWICHES

Chicken Parmigiana Sandwiches

The recipe for this "chicken Parm" sandwich is the same as that for a plate of chicken parmigiana (page 156), with the addition of distinctively Italian focaccia bread in which to nestle the chicken. Needless to say, if you can't get this particular bread, others will work. But make sure whatever kind you use is sturdy enough so as not to disintegrate under the weight and sauce of this hearty preparation.

1½ cups breadcrumbs	3 cups meat sauce (see page 82)
½ teaspoon oregano	½ cup grated Parmesan cheese
½ teaspoon basil	½ cup grated Romano cheese
½ teaspoon salt	12 (2-ounce) slices mozzarella cheese
½ teaspoon pepper	6 (5-inch) tomato focaccia buns
1 teaspoon granulated garlic	
6 (7-ounce) skinless, boneless chicken breasts	
1 cup flour	
1 cup beaten eggs	
1 cup olive oil	

Preheat the oven to 400°F. Combine the breadcrumbs, oregano, basil, salt, pepper, and garlic. Dredge the chicken breasts in the flour, then the beaten eggs, then the seasoned breadcrumbs. Heat the olive oil over medium-high heat in a large sauté pan. Sauté the breaded chicken breasts on each side until golden brown, 2½ to 3 minutes per side. (You may have to sauté the chicken breasts in two batches.) Heat the meat sauce in a medium pot over medium heat. Place the chicken in a baking dish and cover with the meat sauce. Sprinkle the Parmesan and Romano cheeses on each breast. Place 2 slices of mozzarella on each chicken breast and bake in the oven for 6 to 8 minutes or until the chicken reaches an internal temperature of 155°F. Place a chicken breast on each focaccia bun and serve.

MAKES 6 SANDWICHES

Grilled Yellowfin Tuna (Ahi) Sandwiches

Tuna sandwich to some means tuna *salad* sandwich, in which canned tuna is blended with mayonnaise or Miracle Whip. Well *this* tuna sandwich does have mayo in it, but only as a garnish for medium-rare grilled fillets of fresh tuna. It's an entirely different culinary entity.

1	teaspoon curry powder
⅓	cup mayonnaise
½	cup finely diced tomatoes
¼	cup finely diced red onions
1	tablespoon chopped cilantro
4	(6-ounce) fillets yellowfin tuna (ahi)
¼	cup olive oil
	Salt and black pepper
8	thick slices potato bread
8	pieces washed frisée lettuce

Mix the curry powder with the mayonnaise to create a curry mayonnaise. In a small mixing bowl, toss the tomatoes, red onions, and cilantro together to make a relish. Coat the tuna fillets in the olive oil and season with the salt and pepper to taste. Grill or broil the tuna fillets until the desired temperature. (The chef recommends medium rare.) Grill or toast the potato bread. Spread the curry mayonnaise onto the potato bread and place the tuna on the bottom slice of the sandwich. Top with the lettuce and relish. Add the top slice to the sandwich and cut the sandwich on a diagonal. Serve promptly.

MAKES 4 SANDWICHES

CUB FAN BUD MAN

Harry Caray started his broadcast career of over a half century as the voice of the St. Louis Cardinals; he subsequently spent a decade with the Chicago White Sox; but it was his tenure in the broadcast booth with the Chicago Cubs from 1982 to his death in 1998 for which he is best remembered. "I'm a Bud Man and Cubs Fan and I hope you are, too!" Harry used to say; and his ID as Cub Fan Bud Man became four words that many Cubs fans made a virtual mantra.

Harry was an old-fashioned baseball fan who seemed to be an especially good fit with the Cubs and their beautiful, grass-field ball park, Wrigley Field. (For years after every other major league stadium had installed lights for night games, Wrigley Field resisted, and baseball there remained a daytime ritual. Harry was all against lights being installed, and once they were, he was known to grumble about it.) To Harry and to the fans who came to consider him part of their sports family, Wrigley Field seemed like his home; and what he did in the broadcast booth was sometimes as compelling to fans as what was happening on the diamond. He insisted that the booth from which he gave the play-by-play be windowless, even in April when temperatures sometimes dropped to freezing and the wind whipped in off Lake Michigan; and there was no air conditioning during the sweltering summer days. He wanted a feel for the game and to be with the fans, not cut off from them in a temperature-controlled booth.

There is some irony to the fact that Harry died in February 1998 because later that year the Cubs had their finest season in decades, the season in which Sammy Sosa hit sixty-six homers in his duel with Mark McGwire. To honor Harry that year, the team members all wore a caricature of Harry—part of the restaurant's logo—on their uniforms. (The caricature went up over the broadcast booth at Wrigley Field and is still there to this day.) And Harry's tradition of leading the stadium in singing "Take Me Out to the Ball Game" during the seventh-inning stretch was continued by legions of invited celebrities.

In 2000, the Cubs played the Mets in a regular-season game in Japan. Because of the time-zone difference, Harry Caray's restaurant opened at 3:45 A.M.; the downtown restaurant and the branch out in Rosemont were proclaimed "The Two Official Broadcast Locations in the Western Hemisphere to watch the Cubs game." One can only imagine the glee with which Harry would have participated in such an event. Staying up and partying long into the night were second nature to the man. More than one thousand people showed up at the restaurant before dawn to be present for that game; and the kitchen ran so low on eggs that employees scurried out to several White Hen stores for emergency supplies.

In 1999, on the first anniversary of Harry's passing, the restaurant hosted a worldwide simultaneous toast during which fans in bars and eateries from fifty states and fifty countries around the world all simultaneously raised their glasses. "That first year we wanted to get at least seventy-three thousand people," Grant DePorter remembers. "That's how many Budweisers Harry said he drank during his lifetime. In fact, it is estimated that 372,000 people all raised their glasses at the same time." Now, every February, to commemorate Harry's death, the restaurant continues to host a simultaneous worldwide toast to the original Cub Fan Bud Man.

Roasted Turkey Club Sandwiches

You know how there's always more bread than meat in a club sandwich? Not true of this one! Each sandwich contains four slices of bacon as well as six ounces of turkey and only two slices of bread. When cooking the bacon, try to make it crisp but not too brittle. You want it to bend a little as the sandwich gets eaten, not shatter into smithereens.

½   cup mayonnaise
1   tablespoon Dijon mustard
8   slices toasted whole wheat bread
1½ pounds roasted turkey breast
16 slices crispy cooked bacon
8   leaves green leaf lettuce
8   (¼-inch) slices beefsteak tomato

In a small bowl, combine the mayonnaise and Dijon mustard to make Dijon mayonnaise. Spread the Dijon mayonnaise on all the slices of bread. Build each sandwich by piling turkey on top of 1 slice of bread and topping it with 4 slices of bacon, 2 pieces of leaf lettuce, and 2 slices of tomato. Place another piece of bread on the top to finish. Repeat with the remaining ingredients and slice each sandwich on a diagonal to serve.

MAKES 4 SANDWICHES

Chicken Vesuvio Sandwiches

Since there is no Cordon Bleu canon that dictates how to make and serve chicken Vesuvio, it makes sense that Chicago restaurants would invent various ways of enjoying the flavor combinations of which the dish is composed. Harry's Vesuvio sandwich adds Asiago cheese and tomatoes to the mix and deletes the potatoes and peas.

4   (7-ounce) skinless, boneless chicken breasts

1   teaspoon salt

½   teaspoon pepper

2   teaspoons granulated garlic

1   teaspoon oregano

1   teaspoon chopped parsley

¼   cup olive oil

½   cup white wine

½   cup homemade chicken stock (page 94),
     or equivalent amount canned low-sodium chicken broth

4   (2-ounce) slices of Asiago cheese

4   tomato focaccia buns, sliced

4   leaves green leaf lettuce

2   vine-ripened tomatoes, cut into 4 slices each

Season the chicken breasts with the salt, pepper, garlic, oregano, and parsley. Heat a sauté pan over medium heat. Add the olive oil and sauté the chicken breasts on each side until golden brown, 2½ to 3 minutes per side. Deglaze the pan with the wine. Add the chicken stock and simmer until the chicken is cooked to an internal temperature of 155°F. Place a slice of Asiago cheese on each chicken breast and melt. Remove each chicken breast from the pan and place it on the bottom slice of a focaccia bun. Top each chicken breast with a lettuce leaf and two tomato slices. Take the tops of the focaccia buns and dip the underside in the remaining pan juices. Place on top of the sandwiches and serve.

MAKES 4 SANDWICHES

Grilled New York Strip Sirloin Sandwiches

What's known as a New York Strip steak in Chicago is elsewhere called a Kansas City sirloin, a Delmonico steak, or shell steak. It is cut from the boneless short loin and is, in essence, a Porterhouse without the tenderloin and the bone. It is a superb sandwich that may be easier to eat with a knife and fork.

4   (8-ounce) New York strip steaks, trimmed of fat
    Lawry's seasoned salt
    Black pepper
8   (1½-ounce) slices smoked mozzarella cheese
2   tablespoons olive oil
1   large yellow onion, sliced
4   ciabatta rolls

Pound the steaks to ½-inch thickness. Season the steaks well with the seasoned salt and pepper to taste. Grill the steaks to the desired temperature. Top each steak with 2 slices of the smoked mozzarella cheese and melt under the broiler. Heat the olive oil in a sauté pan to medium. Add the sliced onions and sauté until they are translucent. Toast the ciabatta rolls and slice lengthwise. Place a steak on the bottom slice of each roll and top with the sautéed onions and top of the roll.

MAKES 4 SANDWICHES

Pepper-Crusted Beef Medallion Sandwiches

The dressing made by combining puréed roasted red peppers with hollandaise sauce is an inspired complement for peppery beef and arugula. With thick slices of sweet onion, it makes a brawny sandwich indeed!

---

12   (2-ounce) beef tenderloin medallions
     Lawry's seasoned salt
     Cracked black peppercorns
1   tablespoon butter
12   thick red onion slices
¼   cup roasted red peppers
1   cup hollandaise sauce (see page 91)
4   (7-inch) pieces French bread
¾   pound cleaned and stemmed arugula

Lightly pound the beef medallions with a mallet to ½-inch thickness. Season the medallions with the seasoned salt to taste. Lightly press black peppercorns into both sides of the medallions. Grill the beef to the desired temperature. In a medium sauté pan over medium heat, melt the butter. Sauté the onion slices on both sides until they caramelize. Purée the roasted peppers in a blender or food processor. In a small mixing bowl, fold the red pepper purée into the hollandaise until it is completely incorporated.

To assemble the sandwich, slice each bread piece in half and toast it. On the top half of the bread, spread the red pepper hollandaise. Cover with the arugula. On the bottom half of the sandwich, place the beef medallions and top them with the onion slices. Put the two halves together and serve immediately.

MAKES 4 SANDWICHES

Italian Meatball Sandwiches

Italy is one of the world's great bread countries; and meatballs have symbolized Italian food (for better and for worse) for longer than a century. But it's a pretty safe bet that it was Americans, not Italians, who thought of combining the two elements into a meatball sandwich. Italy's sandwiches (there known as *panini*, i.e. little breads) are little more than afternoon snacks. A great tubular meatball sandwich is a mighty meal.

---

1   clove garlic, chopped

¼   cup butter, softened

4   small crusty Italian loaves, sliced lengthwise

8   Italian meatballs (see page 69)

1   green pepper, roasted and julienned (see page 54 for roasting directions)

1   cup marinara sauce (see page 81)

8   thin slices smoked mozzarella cheese

Preheat the oven to broil. In a small bowl, combine the garlic and butter. Brush the inside of the loaves with the garlic butter mixture. Toast the bread on a cookie sheet under the broiler until it turns golden. Cut the meatballs in half and place four halves along the bottom of each loaf. Top with the green pepper, marinara sauce, and 2 slices of the cheese. Place the sandwiches back under the broiler long enough to melt the cheese. Close the sandwich loaves and serve immediately.

MAKES 4 SANDWICHES

· APPETIZERS ·

Harry's Bruschetta

Savory Italian Cheese Platter

Grilled Marinated Octopus
with Spicy Infused Olive Oil

Jumbo Lump Crab Cakes

Jumbo Shrimp Cocktail

Roasted Red Peppers

Baked Clams

Antipasto Platter

Mozzarella Marinara

Mussels Marinara

Mussels Steamed in Garlic

Shrimp Marsala

Asparagus with Prosciutto and Gorgonzola
in Peppercorn Vinaigrette

Prosciutto and Melon

Beef Carpaccio with Porcini Mushrooms
and Roasted Red Pepper Relish

Sweet Italian Cheese Platter

Harry's Bruschetta

Bruscare means "to roast over coal," and bruschetta refers to toast made by rubbing bread with garlic cloves and olive oil, then grilling or toasting it. Tomato, peppers, and olives are traditional bruschetta toppings.

6	beefsteak tomatoes
⅓	plus ¼ cup extra virgin olive oil
1	teaspoon chopped garlic
1	(12-inch) loaf crusty Italian bread, cut into ¾-inch slices
¼	cup balsamic vinegar
¼	cup red wine vinegar
2	tablespoons chopped garlic
2	tablespoons chopped fresh basil
	Salt and pepper
½	cup julienned roasted red peppers
6	kalamata olives
¼	cup shaved Parmigiano-Reggiano cheese

To prepare the tomatoes, core them and score the top with an X. To blanch the tomatoes, place them in boiling water for 1 minute and then immediately transfer the tomatoes to an ice bath. Peel off the skins of the tomatoes, remove the seeds, and dice them into ¾-inch pieces. In a medium bowl, toss the tomatoes, ⅓ cup olive oil, balsamic vinegar, red wine vinegar, garlic, basil, and salt and pepper to taste. Marinate in the refrigerator for ½ hour. In a small bowl, combine the remaining olive oil and garlic. Brush the bread slices with the mixture and toast or grill them. Just prior to serving, warm the bread slices in the oven. Place the tomato mixture in the center of a large round platter. Arrange the bread slices around the tomatoes and garnish with the roasted red pepper and olives. Sprinkle the Parmigiano-Reggiano on top of the tomatoes and serve.

MAKES 4 SERVINGS

Savory Italian Cheese Platter

It used to be that when people thought of Italian cheese, they automatically thought of cheese-flavored powder in a can or maybe bland shredded mozzarella for a pizza. Here's a quartet of superior cheeses with peppers and olives for side-bites and vivid vinegar to bring out their dairy richness. Romano is the best of the Pecorinos, a *piccante* cheese pressed from sheep's milk; Gorgonzola, made in Lombardy, is known for the spicy blue veins of greenish-blue mold that contrast with its creamy paste; Provolone is smooth and fine-textured with a smoky snap and is made from cow's milk; and mozzarella, at its best, is soft and creamy.

---

4   ounces Pecorino Romano cheese

4   ounces Gorgonzola cheese

4   ounces provolone cheese

4   ounces sliced fresh mozzarella cheese
     (Buffalo mozzarella is best, but hard to find.)

½   cup roasted red peppers

5   to 6 pepperoncini

5   to 6 kalamata olives
     Balsamic vinegar

On a medium-size, square cheese platter, arrange large hunks of the Pecorino Romano, the Gorgonzola, and the provolone in three of the corners of the platter. In the fourth corner, arrange the sliced mozzarella. Mound the roasted red peppers in the center of the platter. Arrange the Tuscan peppers around the red peppers and scatter the kalamata olives around the platter. Drizzle the entire platter with the balsamic vinegar. Serve with crackers or warm bread.

MAKES 4 SERVINGS

Grilled Marinated Octopus with Spicy Infused Olive Oil

When marinated overnight and grilled quickly, then served immediately, octopus is melt-in-the-mouth tender.

FOR THE MARINADE:

1½ cups olive oil

1 teaspoon salt

½ teaspoon black pepper

1 tablespoon fresh rosemary
    Juice of 1 lemon

6 cloves garlic, finely chopped

½ teaspoon crushed red pepper

½ tablespoon chopped parsley

FOR THE DISH:

4 (8- to 10-ounce) cleaned baby octopuses, marinated

1 cup roughly chopped radicchio

1 cup roughly chopped hearts of romaine

6 lemon wedges

To make the marinade, combine the olive oil, salt, pepper, rosemary, lemon juice, garlic, red pepper, and parsley. Cover the octopus with the marinade and refrigerate overnight.

To make the dish, the octopus needs to be cooked very fast with high heat in order to keep it from getting too tough. If cooking the octopus on a grill, make sure the grill is as hot as possible. If cooking the octopus under the broiler, use the top shelf. Cook the octopus for 3 minutes on each side. At the same time, place the leftover marinade into a pie tin and place it under the broiler to heat. Slice the cooked octopus into bite-size pieces and arrange on a platter over the roughly cut radicchio and hearts of romaine. Take the heated marinade and drizzle it over the top of the octopus. Garnish with the lemon wedges. Serve promptly.

MAKES 6 SERVINGS

Jumbo Lump Crab Cakes

Jumbo lump crab meat is the best there is, picked from the hind leg area of the blue claw crab or swimmer crab. The chunky sweet meat is the only kind Harry Caray's kitchen uses for its outstanding crab cakes.

¼	cup finely diced red onion
¼	cup finely diced red and yellow pepper
2	tablespoons thinly sliced scallions
¾	cup Japanese breadcrumbs (Panko)
½	cup heavy cream
1	tablespoon Dijon mustard
1	teaspoon Worcestershire sauce
1	teaspoon Tabasco
1	teaspoon Old Bay Seasoning
½	teaspoon granulated garlic
1	egg
1	egg yolk
	Salt and pepper
2	tablespoons lemon juice
1½	pounds jumbo lump blue crabmeat
⅓	stick butter
½	cup flour
2	cups rémoulade sauce (see page 87)

In a large mixing bowl, combine the red onion, peppers, scallions, breadcrumbs, heavy cream, Dijon mustard, Worcestershire, Tabasco, Old Bay, garlic, egg, egg yolk, salt and pepper to taste, and lemon juice. Gently fold in the crabmeat, being careful to not break up the lumps. Form into 3-ounce patties. Preheat the oven to 400°F. In a sauté pan, melt the butter over medium heat. Lightly dust the crab cakes with flour so they don't stick to the pan. Brown the crab cakes on each side, about 1 minute per side, and then bake the cakes in the oven for 5 to 7 minutes. Serve with the rémoulade sauce.

MAKES 12 (3-OUNCE) CRAB CAKES

Jumbo Shrimp Cocktail

When you buy shrimp it is classified in different sizes. The size is determined by how many are in a pound. Harry Caray's uses U12s (less than twelve per pound), which are some of the largest you can buy.

1   *gallon water*

1   *tablespoon pickling spice*

1   *lemon, quartered*

1½ *pounds (size U12) headless, shells-on shrimp*

6   *radicchio leaves*

1½ *cups cocktail sauce (see page 89)*

3   *teaspoons prepared horseradish*

1   *lemon, cut into 6 wheels*

6   *parsley sprigs*

In a large stockpot, combine the water and the pickling spice. Squeeze the lemon into the water and then drop the lemon pieces into the water. Bring the mixture to a boil over high heat. Add the shrimp and cook for 5 to 8 minutes, or until the shrimp are white all the way through. Remove the shrimp from the heat and immediately immerse in cold water to stop the cooking process. Peel and devein the shrimp, leaving the tail on. Serve in six individual parfait glasses. Place 1 leaf of radicchio in the bottom of each glass. Cover the leaf with the cocktail sauce. Hang 4 or 5 shrimp around the rim of each glass with the tails hanging over the outside of the glass. Add ½ teaspoon of horseradish to the center of the cocktail sauce. Garnish with a wheel of lemon on the rim of the glass and a parsley sprig.

MAKES 6 SERVINGS

Roasted Red Peppers

Although roasted red peppers are available on supermarket shelves, when you make them yourself you get a smoky, intense vegetable flavor that the jarred ones cannot match. Be sure to peel away all the charred skin and remove all seeds.

6   *extra large red peppers*
1   *cup Italian vinaigrette (see page 100)*
12 *large basil leaves*
12 *kalamata olives*
12 *anchovy fillets*

To roast the peppers, take each pepper with a pair of tongs and hold it over a medium flame (or coat them with oil and broil them in the oven), turning the pepper until the skin is blackened on all sides. Immediately place the blackened peppers in a large, sealable plastic bag and allow them to sit at room temperature for 30 minutes. Remove the peppers from the bag, peel away the blackened skin, and remove the seeds. Cut the peppers into 1½-inch-wide strips.

In a medium bowl, toss the roasted peppers with the Italian dressing. Refrigerate for a minimum of 1 hour. To serve, arrange the roasted peppers, basil leaves, olives, and anchovies on a platter.

MAKES 4 TO 6 SERVINGS

Baked Clams

The smaller the hard-shell clam, the more tender it is. Littlenecks, or top necks, freshly opened and properly prepared, are little nuggets of bright marine flavor that combine magically with garlic, breadcrumbs, white wine, and spice.

FOR THE CLAM BUTTER:

1   pound softened butter
1   tablespoon chopped garlic
1   teaspoon parsley
1   teaspoon chopped scallions
¼   teaspoon Tabasco
½   teaspoon Worcestershire sauce
1   tablespoon white wine
½   cup breadcrumbs
    Salt and white pepper

FOR THE DISH:

2   dozen fresh top-neck clams
½   cup breadcrumbs
1   cup clam juice
¼   teaspoon paprika
½   tablespoon chopped fresh parsley
1   lemon, cut into 6 wedges
    Sprig of fresh parsley

To make the clam butter, combine the softened butter with the garlic, 1 teaspoon parsley, scallions, Tabasco, Worcestershire, white wine, ½ cup breadcrumbs, and salt and pepper to taste. Roll the mixture into a log 1 inch in diameter, wrap it in wax paper, and refrigerate. The clam butter can also be frozen.

Preheat the oven to 400°F. For the dish, rinse the clams and shuck them open, making sure to separate the clam completely from the shell. Discard the top shell and keep the clam sitting in the bottom shell. Place the clams on the half shell in a shallow baking dish. Top each clam with a ¼-inch slice of the clam butter. In the center of the baking dish, spread the remaining ½ cup breadcrumbs and top them with 6 slices of the clam butter to create a sauce for the clams. Pour the clam juice into the baking dish and sprinkle the clams and the sauce with the paprika and the remaining ½ tablespoon chopped parsley. Bake the clams in the oven for approximately 12 to 15 minutes. Do not overcook the clams or they will become tough. To serve, spread the breadcrumb sauce in the center of a large platter and arrange the baked clams around the outside. Garnish the platter with the lemon wedges and the sprig of parsley.

MAKES 4 TO 6 SERVINGS

THE CHICAGO WAY TO EAT

Some recipes are unique to Chicago. Chicken Vesuvio, shrimp de Jonghe, and the Italian beef sandwich are three such signature dishes served at Harry Caray's; but it isn't so much *what* Harry Caray's serves that makes its meals so definitively Chicago; it's *how* they're served. Nothing is small.

Garrick Dickie, who started with the company in 1990 and is now corporate chef, said, "It is the Chicago tradition to serve everything twice its size. Large portions are the way people in this city expect to eat when they go out. The guest who comes to this restaurant [is looking for] a big steak and a potato to go with it."

The potatoes are immense: "40 count" spuds, meaning that a fifty-pound case contains forty of them, and that each one, baked and served, is nearly the size of a small rye bread loaf. The one-pound Sicilian-style veal chop is more than an inch thick and encompasses the plate. At lunch if you want a hamburger, the "Holy Cow!" burger is flabbergasting: a ten-ounce hunk of freshly ground beef heaped with cheddar cheese, grilled onions, and sautéed mushrooms. And you are reminded if you order the signature chicken Vesuvio that one theory of how this mighty dish got named is that it looks like a volcano when served: a veritable mountain of chicken and tender sections of potato overflowing with garlicky juices.

"There is a lot of sharing at the tables in this place," Garrick reminded us, pointing to the fact that every table in the restaurant comes with a tall stack of small plates suitable for splitting dishes and passing tastes of everything around. That's the Chicago way to eat.

Antipasto Platter

Shoppers no longer need to hunt down a *salumeria* or pork store in the Italian part of town to find meats for a good antipasto platter. Such once-exotic salamis and sausages are found in many good supermarket deli cases. Of course the *best* meats are still found behind the counter of true Italian butchers.

¼ pound thinly sliced spicy soppressata

¼ pound thinly sliced Genoa salami

¼ pound thinly sliced cured coppa

¼ pound thinly sliced mortadella

¼ pound thinly sliced provolone cheese

⅓ cup chopped hearts of palm

½ cup quartered artichoke hearts

8 pepperoncini

8 anchovy fillets

8 green onions

½ cantaloupe, peeled and seeded

8 thin slices prosciutto

1 red pepper, julienned

8 fresh basil leaves

8 kalamata olives

1½ tablespoons extra virgin olive oil

On a large round platter, arrange the sliced soppressata, salami, coppa, mortadella, and the provolone cheese covering the bottom of the entire platter. Equally distribute the hearts of palm, artichoke hearts, pepperoncini, and the anchovies around the platter on top of the meats and cheese. Clean the green onions. Slice the green end of the onions lengthwise to create a fan. Arrange the onions symmetrically on the platter. Slice the cantaloupe into 8 wedges and wrap each wedge with 1 slice of prosciutto. Arrange the cantaloupe symmetrically on the platter. Garnish the platter with the julienned red pepper, basil leaves, and kalamata olives. Drizzle the platter with the olive oil.

MAKES 8 SERVINGS

Mozzarella Marinara

Served warm with marinara sauce for dipping, fried nuggets of mozzarella cheese are a creamy-centered hors d'oeuvre.

---

8   eggs

2   pounds mozzarella cheese, sliced ¼ inch thick

1   cup flour

2   cups breadcrumbs

2   cups peanut or canola oil

1½   cups marinara sauce (see page 81)

Whisk the eggs in a medium bowl. Cut the mozzarella into 1 x 2-inch pieces and dredge them first in the flour, then in the egg, and then in the breadcrumbs. Refrigerate for 10 to 15 minutes. Take the breaded mozzarella slices and dip them into the egg again and then into the breadcrumbs again. Heat the oil in a large sauté pan over medium-high heat. Fry the mozzarella slices in the hot oil, turning once, until golden brown, 1 to 2 minutes per side. Serve with the marinara sauce for dipping.

MAKES 6 TO 8 SERVINGS

Mussels Marinara

When buying mussels, get live ones and keep them refrigerated in a container that allows them to breathe until ready to use. Scrub them well and debeard them by pulling the weedy protrusion out from between the shells. Don't debeard them until right before cooking. Discard any that don't open when cooked.

3   pounds fresh Mediterranean black mussels, cleaned
¼   cup olive oil
1   cup clam juice
⅓   cup chopped scallions
1   teaspoon oregano
2   tablespoons chopped fresh garlic
1½ cups marinara sauce (see page 81)
    Salt and pepper
1   tablespoon chopped parsley

In a large stockpot, combine the mussels, olive oil, clam juice, scallions, oregano, garlic, and the marinara sauce. Bring the mixture to a boil, and then reduce the heat and simmer, stirring occasionally, until the mussels open, 6 to 8 minutes. Add the salt and pepper to taste. Pour the mussel mixture into individual bowls. Garnish each bowl with the chopped parsley.

MAKES 4 TO 6 SERVINGS

Mussels Steamed in Garlic

This dish is focused on mussels. Don't debeard them until right before cooking. Discard any that don't open when cooked. It is for seafood lovers only. Serve it with thick slabs of crusty Italian bread for mopping all the juice from the bowl.

3 pounds fresh Mediterranean black mussels, cleaned
¼ cup olive oil
1 cup clam juice
1 cup white wine
½ cup chopped scallions
1 teaspoon oregano
2 tablespoons chopped fresh garlic
   Salt and pepper
1 tablespoon chopped parsley

In a large stockpot, combine the mussels, olive oil, clam juice, white wine, scallions, oregano, and garlic. Bring the mixture to a boil, and then reduce the heat and simmer, stirring occasionally, until the mussels open, 6 to 8 minutes. Add the salt and pepper to taste. Pour the mussel mixture into individual bowls. Garnish each bowl with chopped parsley.

MAKES 4 TO 6 SERVINGS

Shrimp Marsala

A tremendously aromatic dish that makes either an appetizer or, with a baked potato and green vegetable on the side, a satisfying main course.

---

12 (size U12) headless, shell-on shrimp

⅓ cup butter

¼ cup flour

16 red grapes

1 tablespoon chopped garlic

½ cup Marsala wine

½ cup homemade chicken stock (page 94),
    or equivalent amount canned low-sodium chicken broth

1 teaspoon chopped parsley

Peel, devein, and butterfly the shrimp. In a large sauté pan, melt the butter over medium heat. Dredge the shrimp in the flour and sauté with the red grapes and garlic in the butter until the garlic turns brown. Remove from the heat and deglaze the pan with the Marsala wine. Return to the heat and reduce by one-third. Add the chicken stock, reduce the heat, and simmer until the sauce reduces by one-half. Serve on a platter and garnish with chopped parsley.

MAKES 4 SERVINGS

Asparagus with Prosciutto and Gorgonzola in Peppercorn Vinaigrette

Salty prosciutto, luxurious Gorgonzola, and briny olives all help amplify the earthy vegetable flavor of al dente asparagus stalks.

FOR THE PEPPERCORN VINAIGRETTE:

½   cup olive oil

2   tablespoons balsamic vinegar

2   tablespoons red wine vinegar

½   tablespoon chopped fresh garlic

1   tablespoon cracked black peppercorns

½   tablespoon diced shallots

1   teaspoon chopped basil

½   teaspoon salt

FOR THE DISH:

6   cups water

16 asparagus spears, cleaned and trimmed

¼   pound thinly sliced prosciutto

½   cup crumbled Gorgonzola cheese

4   kalamata olives

2   sprigs parsley

½   red pepper, julienned

To make the peppercorn vinaigrette, combine the olive oil, balsamic vinegar, red wine vinegar, garlic, peppercorns, shallots, basil, and salt in a small mixing bowl. Whisk together and refrigerate until needed.

Put the water in a medium stockpot over high heat and bring to a boil. Drop the asparagus in the boiling water for 2 minutes, strain off the liquid, and rinse with cold water. Chill the asparagus. Arrange the asparagus in the center of a medium-size serving platter. Fold the prosciutto slices over the ends of the asparagus. Sprinkle the Gorgonzola cheese over the tips of the asparagus. Drizzle the peppercorn vinaigrette over the asparagus, prosciutto, and Gorgonzola. Garnish the platter with the olives, parsley sprigs, and julienned red pepper.

MAKES 4 SERVINGS

Prosciutto and Melon

The flavor of this dish depends entirely on quality and condition of ingredients. Top-quality prosciutto, sliced very thin and brought to room temperature, has a saline kick that makes ripe cantaloupe taste all the sweeter.

---

1   *cantaloupe, peeled, seeded, and sliced into 6 wedges*

¼   *pound thinly sliced prosciutto*

1   *tablespoon extra virgin olive oil*

6   *kalamata olives*

2   *parsley sprigs*

Slice the cantaloupe wedges lengthwise to ½-inch from the bottom. Spread the wedges into fans. Arrange the cantaloupe fans around the outer edge of a large round platter. Pile the thinly sliced prosciutto in the center of the platter. Drizzle the prosciutto and the melon with the olive oil. Garnish with the olives and parsley sprigs.

MAKES 4 TO 6 SERVINGS

Beef Carpaccio with Porcini Mushrooms and Roasted Red Pepper Relish

Beef carpaccio was first served in Venice at Harry's Bar. It was named for Renaissance painter Vittore Carpaccio, known for the profusion of red in his paintings. Beef Carpaccio is indeed bright red because it is raw beef.

FOR THE RELISH:

1   tablespoon olive oil

¼   pound dried porcini mushrooms, re-hydrated and sliced

1   roasted red pepper, peeled, seeded, and julienned

2   tablespoons extra virgin olive oil

1   tablespoon balsamic vinegar

3   sprigs fresh parsley, finely chopped

    Salt and pepper

FOR THE CARPACCIO:

6   ounces sliced beef tenderloin, pounded thin

2   sprigs fresh watercress

1   teaspoon extra virgin olive oil

¼   teaspoon cracked black peppercorns

¼   teaspoon kosher salt

¼   cup grated Parmigiano-Reggiano cheese

To make the relish, heat the olive oil over medium-high heat and sauté the porcini mushrooms until they are soft. Set aside and allow to cool. In a medium mixing bowl, combine the mushrooms, red peppers, olive oil, vinegar, and parsley. Season the relish with salt and pepper to taste.

To make the carpaccio, arrange the thinly pounded tenderloin in the center of the plate in a loose mound. Top the tenderloin with the mushroom and pepper relish. Garnish with the watercress sprigs. Drizzle the olive oil around the plate and finish it with the peppercorns, kosher salt, and grated Parmigiano-Reggiano. Serve cold.

MAKES 4 SERVINGS

Sweet Italian Cheese Platter

For those with a serious sweet tooth who aren't interested in frilly cakes and puddings, a platter of cheeses adorned with liquor-infused fruits and sugar-toasted nuts is deliriously satisfying. Because it is so sweet, this is often served as a dessert.

6	fresh figs
¼	cup bourbon
6	dried apricots
¼	cup brandy
1	tablespoon butter
¼	cup brown sugar
¼	cup walnut halves
1	pear, cored and sliced
1	cup balsamic vinegar

4	ounces sliced fresh mozzarella cheese (Buffalo mozzarella is best, but hard to find.)
4	ounces Pecorino Romano cheese
4	ounces Gorgonzola cheese
4	ounces provolone cheese

Cut the figs in half and soak them in the bourbon overnight. Soak the apricots in the brandy overnight. Preheat the oven to 350°F. In a sauté pan, melt the butter over medium heat and stir in the brown sugar until dissolved. Toss the walnuts in the brown sugar mixture. Remove the walnuts, reserving the brown sugar mixture, and place the walnuts on a cookie sheet. Bake them in the oven for 10 to 15 minutes or until the walnuts are crisp. Add the pear slices to the brown sugar mixture and sauté over medium heat until the pears are caramelized. Heat the balsamic vinegar in a small pot over medium heat. Reduce the vinegar by two-thirds until it reaches a syrupy consistency.

To assemble the platter, on a medium-size square cheese platter, arrange large hunks of the Pecorino Romano, the Gorgonzola, and the provolone in three of the corners of the platter. In the fourth corner, arrange the sliced mozzarella. In the center of the cheese, arrange the bourbon-soaked figs, the brandy-soaked apricots, and the caramelized pears. Scatter the candied walnuts around the platter. Drizzle the balsamic reduction over the entire platter. Serve with crackers or warm bread.

MAKES 4 SERVINGS

• SIDE DISHES •

Homemade Italian Meatballs

Sautéed Spinach with Garlic and Oil

Garlic Mashed Potatoes

Vesuvio Potatoes

Sautéed Mushrooms

*Sautéed Broccoli and Mushrooms
with Garlic*

Creamed Spinach

Grilled Asparagus

Homemade Italian Meatballs

Beef-and-pork *polpette* (meatballs) freeze well, so you can always have a supply on hand. These meatballs go with almost any pasta, or make a wonderful dish by themselves, topped with the best marinara or meat sauce.

2	pounds ground beef
1	pound ground pork
⅓	cup finely diced yellow onion
⅓	cup finely diced green pepper
¼	cup ketchup
⅓	cup tomato juice
1	tablespoon Worcestershire sauce
	Dash of Tabasco
2	tablespoons grated Parmesan cheese
2	tablespoons grated Romano cheese
4	tablespoons breadcrumbs
1	tablespoon chopped parsley
3	eggs
1	teaspoon salt
½	teaspoon black pepper

Preheat the oven to 350°F. In a large mixing bowl, combine the ground beef, ground pork, onion, and green pepper together. Mix thoroughly. Add the ketchup, tomato juice, Worcestershire sauce, Tabasco, Parmesan cheese, Romano cheese, breadcrumbs, parsley, eggs, salt, and pepper. Mix thoroughly together. Form the mixture into 3-ounce balls, slightly larger than a golf ball, and place on a cookie sheet. Bake in the oven for approximately 20 to 30 minutes, or until the meatballs reach an internal temperature of 140°F. Rotate the cookie sheet in the oven halfway through the baking process.

MAKES APPROXIMATELY 20 MEATBALLS

Sautéed Spinach with Garlic and Oil

Most of America's best steakhouses offer excellent spinach dishes because the leafy green vegetable is such a perfect complement for prime steak. Harry Caray's version is powerfully garlicked.

8   cups of water
1   pound fresh spinach, cleaned and stemmed
2   tablespoons olive oil
1   tablespoon finely chopped fresh garlic
    Salt and black pepper

Put the water in a medium stockpot over high heat and bring to a boil. Drop the spinach in the boiling water and immediately strain off the liquid and rinse with cold water. Squeeze off the excess water. Heat a sauté pan to medium and add the olive oil, garlic, and spinach. Sauté for 1 minute. Add the salt and black pepper to taste.

MAKES 4 SERVINGS

Garlic Mashed Potatoes

The only two reasons we would consider NOT ordering garlic mashed potatoes with a Harry Caray's steak are the alternative Vesuvio potatoes and the huge baked potatoes that are also available. Despite such temptations, mashed spuds are impossible to resist, especially if you get a whiff of an order being carried from the kitchen past your table.

6   large Idaho russet potatoes, peeled
8   cloves garlic, peeled
6   cups homemade chicken stock (see page 94),
    or equivalent amount canned low-sodium chicken broth
¼   pound (1 stick) butter
1   teaspoon granulated garlic, or to taste
1   cup heavy cream
    Salt and white pepper

In a medium stockpot, combine the potatoes, garlic cloves, and enough chicken stock to float the potatoes 2 inches off the bottom of the pot. Bring to a low boil for 40 minutes or until you can easily separate the potatoes with a fork. Strain off the liquid and add the butter and granulated garlic. Mash the potatoes, adding the heavy cream until the mixture reaches the desired consistency. Add salt and white pepper to taste.

MAKES 6 SERVINGS

Vesuvio Potatoes

Alongside almost any beef or chicken dish, and with sturdy slabs of fish, Vesuvio potatoes provide a hearty contrast.

4	large Idaho russet potatoes
¼	cup olive oil
6	cloves whole garlic
½	teaspoon salt
¼	teaspoon pepper
1½	teaspoons oregano
2	teaspoons granulated garlic
2	tablespoons chopped parsley
⅔	cup white wine
⅔	cup homemade chicken stock (page 94), or equivalent amount canned low-sodium chicken broth

---

Preheat the oven to 400°F. Peel the potatoes and cut them into quarters lengthwise. In a large roasting pan, heat the olive oil over medium heat. Add the potatoes and garlic cloves and sauté the potatoes until golden brown. Remove the garlic cloves from the pan and discard. Pour off half of the oil from the pan. Season the potatoes with the salt, pepper, oregano, granulated garlic, and parsley. Deglaze the pan with the wine. Add the chicken stock and then remove the roasting pan to the oven. Bake in the oven for 12 minutes or until the potatoes become tender. Arrange the potatoes on a large serving platter, cover them with the pan juices, and serve.

MAKES 4 TO 6 SERVINGS

Sautéed Mushrooms

Mushrooms should be sautéed at a leisurely pace and with plenty of olive oil. The long, slow simmer helps them soften and become a top-of-the-line accompaniment for a USDA center cut prime steak.

¼ cup olive oil

2 pounds button mushrooms, cleaned and sliced evenly

1 teaspoon kosher salt

½ teaspoon black pepper

1 tablespoon white wine vinegar

½ tablespoon chopped Italian parsley

Heat the olive oil in a large sauté pan over medium heat. Add the mushrooms, kosher salt, black pepper, and vinegar. Sauté the mixture until the mushrooms turn soft. Serve immediately on a small platter and garnish with the parsley.

MAKES 4 TO 6 SERVINGS

MEMORABILIA ON DISPLAY

People come to Harry Caray's to eat, to talk business, and to shmooze, but whatever brings them in, nearly every guest is sooner or later mesmerized by the fantastic items on display. As much a gallery as it is a restaurant, the four-story building is a treasury of baseball memorabilia. Ranging from Harry's own gigantic black-framed glasses and his 1989 Hall of Fame ring to original vintage newspaper sports pages highlighting some of the greatest moments in baseball history, the collection of keepsakes and clippings is funny, sentimental, and informative.

There are 8 x 10 photos everywhere, some including Harry with celebrities, some inscribed to him from the likes of Jay Leno ("Yo Harry! Thanks for everything!") and Mike Ditka ("Holy Cow! You're the greatest!"). You get to see Harry, young and old, standing alongside Elton John, Ronald Reagan, Bill Murray, Mayor Richard M. Daley, Bill Clinton, and Bozo the Clown. And there are dozens of photos that show Harry at work all during his long career as sportscaster for the St. Louis Cardinals (1945–1969), Oakland A's (1970), Chicago White Sox (1971–1981) and Chicago Cubs (1982–1997). Here, too, are images that tell the history of baseball in Chicago and beyond: photos that show the construction of the Wrigley Field bleachers, images of the original Comiskey Park from its early days to its demolition, portraits by Chicago photographer George Brace of more than two hundred inductees into the Baseball Hall of Fame.

The actual glasses Harry wore every day of his life.

Special highlighted showcases between the hallway and the first floor dining rooms contain the really choice memorabilia from such baseball greats as Stan Musial, Ernie Banks, Ted Williams, Hank Aaron, and Carlton Fisk. Included in these cases are an autographed bat Sammy Sosa used in July of 1998 during his amazing home run streak (twenty in a single month) and Billy Williams's 1972 All-Star Game bat.

Among the unique items on display is one of three Gibson guitars honoring all Cubs Hall of Famers, including Harry Caray—signed by Sammy Sosa, Ryne Sandberg, Chip Caray, former manager Don Baylor, Kerry Wood, Ernie Banks, and Billy Williams. Surely the most unusual *objet d'art* on display is the holy cow. This fiberglass cow, wears big black glasses just like those Harry wore and has

big holes that go all the way through its body. Artist Ken Aiken created it for a 1999 Chicago art event called *Cows on Parade*, for which various artists created all shapes and sizes of different fantasy bovines to display throughout the city.

As you enter the restaurant, you will see four seats from the original Comiskey Park, donated by the White Sox. And you cannot help but be wowed by a larger-than-life white bronze bust of Harry Caray, which was made from the same mold as the full-body, seven-foot-tall statue that graces Wrigley Field. In this instance, however, to give special honor to the man Harry Caray really was, sculptors Omri Amrany and Lou Cella enriched the molten bronze itself with a good measure of material dear to the man they were sculpting: Budweiser beer. To our knowledge, this is the art world's only bust made of bronze and Bud.

Sautéed Broccoli and Mushrooms with Garlic

A longside a plate of pasta with marinara sauce, bright green broccoli creates an inspired Italian flag. Don't overcook; you'll want this broccoli al dente.

4	pounds broccoli
¼	cup olive oil
½	teaspoon salt
¼	teaspoon black pepper
½	teaspoon granulated garlic
	Sautéed mushrooms (see page 73)

To prepare the broccoli, trim away the stems to 1 inch below the florets. Cut into 2- by 2-inch pieces. Bring the water to a boil over high heat. Blanch the florets by placing them in boiling water (about ½ gallon) for 2 to 3 minutes and then rinsing in cold water to stop the cooking. In a large sauté pan over medium heat, heat the olive oil. Transfer the broccoli to the hot oil and season with the salt, pepper, and granulated garlic. Sauté for approximately 2 to 3 minutes.

To prepare the dish, arrange the broccoli heads on a large platter with the heads facing out and the stems toward the center of the dish. Cover the stems with the sautéed mushrooms.

MAKES 4 TO 6 SERVINGS

Creamed Spinach

We love creamed spinach because it is so healthy (hey, it's spinach, right?) and yet it is as rich as butter and cream. A great companion to any kind of beef or chicken, and a good partner with Vesuvio potatoes for a no-meat, high-garlic meal.

⅓ cup heavy cream

2 tablespoons butter

¼ teaspoon ground nutmeg

   Black pepper

1 pound fresh spinach, cleaned and stemmed

¼ cup grated Parmigiano-Reggiano cheese

In a medium saucepan over medium heat, combine the heavy cream, butter, nutmeg, and pepper to taste. Stirring constantly, bring the mixture to a boil. Reduce the heat to a simmer. Blanch the spinach by placing in boiling water for 1 minute and then rinsing with cold water. Squeeze out the excess water. Slowly add the spinach to the heavy cream mixture and return it to a boil. Toss in the cheese, remove from the heat, and serve immediately.

MAKES 4 TO 6 SERVINGS

Grilled Asparagus

You can grill skinny asparagus stalks, but for a full-flavored dish it is best to use big ones, up to a half-inch in diameter. They've got the toothy texture and depth of flavor that holds up to a hot grill and they will cook through without turning to mush.

1½   *pounds jumbo asparagus*

8   *cups water*

¼   *cup olive oil*

½   *teaspoon Lawry's seasoned salt*

¼   *teaspoon black pepper*

Remove three-quarters of an inch of the asparagus stems. With a potato peeler, peel away the skin three-quarter inch up from the bottom of the stem. Bring the water to a boil over high heat. Immerse the asparagus in the water for 2 minutes or until the asparagus begins to become tender. Remove the asparagus and place them in a cold water bath. In a shallow pan, combine the olive oil, seasoned salt, and black pepper. Coat the asparagus in the olive oil mixture. Grill the asparagus for approximately 1 to 2 minutes, turning the asparagus so they are marked on all sides. Serve immediately.

MAKES 4 SERVINGS

SAUCES, STOCKS & DRESSINGS

Marinara Sauce

Meat Sauce

Alfredo Sauce

Arrabbiata Sauce

Pesto Sauce

Aurore Sauce

Rémoulade Sauce

Roasted Red Pepper Cream Sauce

Cocktail Sauce

Brandy Shallot Butter

Clarified Butter

Hollandaise Sauce

Bordelaise Sauce

Homemade Chicken Stock

Homemade Beef Stock

Sun-Dried Tomato Vinaigrette

Sweet Herb Vinaigrette

Raspberry Vinaigrette

Harry's Caesar Dressing

Italian Vinaigrette

Marinara Sauce

No ingredient defines Italian-American cooking as much as marinara. It's the classic, long-simmered red sauce for which every cook has a formula. The significant variables have to do with garlic and tomatoes: how much of the former and what kind of the latter? Whatever the simplicity or complication of its creation, it is a vastly multipurpose sauce, suitable for seafood, pastas, cheeses, meats, and even vegetables.

---

2   *tablespoons chopped garlic*

¼   *cup olive oil*

6   *cups canned plum tomatoes*

⅓   *cup tomato purée*

2   *tablespoons finely chopped fresh basil*

1   *teaspoon granulated garlic*

1   *teaspoon sugar*

      Salt and pepper

In a heavy-bottomed, medium-size stockpot over medium heat, sauté the chopped garlic in the olive oil until brown. Add the tomatoes, tomato purée, basil, garlic, and sugar. Simmer for 1 hour. Add salt and pepper to taste. This can be frozen for future use.

MAKES 6 CUPS

Meat Sauce

Many Italian-Americans refer to meat sauce as "gravy". Simmered long and slow, it is a multipurpose dish that goes on almost any kind of pasta and is especially wonderful when simply "sipped" by spoon from the pot as it cooks.

¼	cup olive oil
½	pound pork neck bones
1	pound ground pork
½	pound ground chuck
⅓	pound skinless salt pork
1	green pepper, diced
½	yellow onion, diced
1½	teaspoons chopped garlic
2	tablespoons fresh chopped basil
½	tablespoon sugar
1	tablespoon granulated garlic
	Salt and pepper
8	cups plum tomatoes
½	cup tomato purée

Heat the olive oil over medium heat in a large, heavy-bottomed stockpot. Add the pork neck bones, ground pork, ground chuck, and salt pork and brown for approximately 5 minutes. Stir in the green pepper, yellow onion, garlic, basil, sugar, granulated garlic and the salt and pepper to taste. Sauté the mixture until the vegetables become translucent. Stir in the plum tomatoes and tomato purée. Simmer over medium heat for at least an hour or until the meat falls off the bone. Strain through a colander; discard the bones and the salt pork.

MAKES 8 TO 10 CUPS

Alfredo Sauce

Butter, cream, cheese, and garlic have become the fundamental ingredients of this rich sauce (which was originally only butter, eggs, and cheese). It is best known for topping fettuccine noodles, but is also great on other pastas as well as on vegetables, chicken, and seafood.

5   tablespoons butter

1⅔ cups heavy cream

½   cup grated Parmesan cheese

½   cup grated Romano cheese

¼   teaspoon salt

¼   teaspoon white pepper

¼   teaspoon granulated garlic

In a large, heavy-bottomed stockpot, combine the butter and cream. Over medium-high heat, bring to a light boil, stirring occasionally. Add the Parmesan and Romano cheeses, stirring continually until the cheeses are incorporated into the sauce. Season the sauce with the salt, white pepper, and granulated garlic. Taste the sauce and add additional salt, white pepper, or granulated garlic as needed.

MAKES 3 TO 4 CUPS

Arrabbiata Sauce

Arrabbiata is derived from the Italian word for "angry." This sauce gets its bite from a fierce fusillade of crushed red pepper flakes.

8   *large beefsteak tomatoes*

⅓   *cup olive oil*

6   *cloves garlic, peeled*

½   *teaspoon crushed red pepper*

¾   *cup finely chopped yellow onion*

2   *tablespoons chopped fresh basil*

   Salt

   White pepper

Core and score the tomatoes by cutting an *X* in the top. Blanch the tomatoes by placing them in boiling water (about 8 cups) until the skins begin to peel away, about 1 to 3 minutes. Immediately transfer the tomatoes to an ice bath and cool them. Peel the skins from the tomatoes. Cut the tomatoes in half crosswise and squeeze them to remove the seeds. Chop the tomatoes into ½-inch squares. In a medium saucepan, heat the olive oil over medium heat. Add the garlic cloves and crushed red pepper and sauté them until the garlic cloves turn brown. Strain the mixture until only the infused olive oil remains. Put the infused oil into a large, heavy-bottomed stockpot over a medium flame. Add the onion and sauté until translucent. Add the tomatoes and basil and bring to a boil. Reduce the heat and simmer the mixture for 45 minutes to 1 hour. Season with the salt and white pepper to taste. Purée the sauce in a blender or food processor. This is a spicy sauce to be tossed with pasta. It can be frozen for later use.

MAKES 4 TO 6 CUPS

Pesto Sauce

Originally from Genoa, Italy, pesto is named for the pestle traditionally used to grind up basil leaves with garlic and pine nuts as the basis of this verdant sauce.

7	*tablespoons extra virgin olive oil*
2	*cups packed fresh basil*
¼	*cup toasted pine nuts*
3	*cloves garlic, peeled and chopped*
½	*tablespoon lemon juice*
¼	*cup grated Parmesan cheese*
	Salt and pepper

Put the olive oil into a blender or food processor. Blend in the fresh basil, pine nuts, chopped garlic, lemon juice, Parmesan cheese, and salt and pepper to taste. Mix until the ingredients are thoroughly blended.

MAKES 1 CUP

Aurore Sauce

A combination of alfredo with marinara sauce, aurore sauce is a kind of pink béchamel suitable for pasta, vegetables, or seafood.

2   *cups marinara sauce (see page 81)*
1   *cup alfredo sauce (see page 83)*
1   *teaspoon chopped fresh thyme (leaves only)*

Heat the marinara sauce in a saucepan over medium heat. Add the alfredo sauce and thyme. Simmer for 5 minutes, stirring frequently.

MAKES 3 CUPS

Rémoulade Sauce

Rémoulade is particularly well suited as the dressing for Jumbo Lump Crab Cakes but can be served as an accompaniment to meat, fish, and shellfish.

---

2   cups mayonnaise

¼   cup chopped capers

¼   cup finely diced red onion

¼   cup Dijon mustard

½   teaspoon Old Bay Seasoning

½   teaspoon paprika

½   tablespoon Worcestershire sauce

½   teaspoon Tabasco

1   teaspoon lemon juice

     Salt and pepper

Combine the mayonnaise, capers, red onion, mustard, Old Bay Seasoning, paprika, Worcestershire, Tabasco, lemon juice, and salt and pepper to taste in a medium bowl.

MAKES 3 CUPS

Roasted Red Pepper Cream Sauce

Wonderful on cheese- or vegetable-filled ravioli!

6   roasted red bell peppers (see page 54)

2   tablespoons olive oil

½   teaspoon sea salt

¼   teaspoon white pepper

1½ cups heavy cream

¼   cup freshly grated Parmigiano-Reggiano cheese

½   tablespoon julienned fresh basil

Purée the red peppers in a blender or food processor. Heat the olive oil in a sauté pan over medium heat and sauté the puréed peppers. Add the salt and pepper. Reduce the heat and gently whisk in the cream and the Parmigiano-Reggiano until they are thoroughly incorporated into the peppers. Stir in the basil and simmer for 5 minutes.

MAKES 3 TO 4 CUPS

Cocktail Sauce

Of course, you want cocktail sauce for shrimp or raw shellfish. But consider also how well it pairs with vegetables or as a complement or sauce for fried calamari or Jumbo Shrimp Cocktail (see page 53).

1	tablespoon finely diced red bell pepper
1	tablespoon finely diced green bell pepper
1	tablespoon finely diced kosher dill pickle
1	tablespoon finely diced celery
1	tablespoon finely diced parsley
2	(8-ounce) bottles Hoffman's Seafood Sauce (or equivalent)
½	cup chili sauce
½	cup ketchup
2	tablespoons lemon juice
1	teaspoon Tabasco
½	teaspoon Worcestershire sauce
	Salt and pepper
¼	cup tomato juice
1	teaspoon prepared horseradish

In a large mixing bowl combine the red bell pepper, green bell pepper, pickle, celery, parsley, seafood sauce, chili sauce, ketchup, lemon juice, Tabasco, Worcestershire, salt and pepper to taste, tomato juice, and horseradish.

MAKES 5 CUPS

Brandy Shallot Butter

The sweetness of the honey and the caramelized shallots make this butter the perfect topping for a warm crusty Italian loaf or bread. This is the butter served with bread at the restaurant.

1 tablespoon clarified butter (see below)
3 shallots, finely diced
1 ounce brandy
1 tablespoon honey
1 pound unsalted butter, softened
   Salt

Heat the clarified butter in a medium sauté pan. Sauté the shallots until they become clear. Set them aside to cool. In a medium mixing bowl combine the brandy, honey, and shallots. Stir in the butter and mix until the ingredients are thoroughly combined. Season with the salt to taste. Refrigerate until ready to use. Spread on crusty Italian bread.

MAKES 1 POUND

Clarified Butter

1 pound unsalted butter

Cut the butter into tablespoon-sized pieces, and melt it slowly over low heat in a deep saucepan. The water in the butter will evaporate, and the milk solids will sink to the bottom. Remove the butter from the heat and skim off the foam that has risen to the surface. Slowly pour the clear melted butter off of the milk solids at the bottom of the saucepan. It may be stored in a jar in the refrigerator or frozen.

Hollandaise Sauce

This is a tricky sauce to get right—it usually takes some time and practice—but what this rich creamy sauce can add to a side of broccoli or asparagus or to seafood dishes makes it worth the effort.

---

8 cups water

4 egg yolks

⅔ cup warm clarified butter (see page 90)

1 tablespoon white wine

½ teaspoon Tabasco

½ teaspoon Worcestershire sauce

1 teaspoon lemon juice

   Salt and white pepper

Bring the water to a simmer in a medium stockpot. Holding a medium stainless steel bowl over the simmering water, whisk the egg yolks until thickened and warm. If the yolks seem to be getting too hot and look like they are beginning to cook, remove them from the heat to a cool surface and whisk until the mixture has cooled very slightly. Put the mixture back over the heat and continue to whisk. When the yolks have tripled in volume and the mixture is very thick and creamy, remove them from the simmering water. Do not overcook the eggs. Slowly whisk in the warm butter. Stabilize the bowl by setting it on a towel. Add the butter slowly in a thin stream, whisking constantly as it is incorporated into the mixture. Season with the wine, Tabasco, Worcestershire, and lemon juice. Add salt and pepper to taste. Serve immediately.

MAKES 1 CUP

FRANK NITTI

Prior to Harry Caray, the biggest name associated with 33 Kinzie Street was Frank "the Enforcer" Nitti, henchman of Al Capone during Prohibition. In 1939, after Capone was jailed and Prohibition was abolished, Frank had become a major figurehead in the Chicago mob. His in-laws, the Caravettas, bought the building that is now home to Harry Caray's restaurant and used it to package and distribute Italian cheeses.

He kept an apartment on the fourth floor, which was, according to Harry Caray's historians, "most definitely a convenient lookout for him. It was near the courthouse building so that he could keep tabs on what was going on around him. The building was also connected to the tunnels running underneath the city, which allowed him to easily leave the building without being seen."

Today, Harry Caray's top floor is used for office space, but Nitti's apartment is intact: cedar closet, bathroom, kitchen, bedroom and living room. The space is decorated with pictures of Nitti, Capone, and other kingpins of early mob days. Behind Nitti's bedroom there is a thick masonry wall with a heavy steel door, leading some curiosity-seekers to wonder if Nitti used this secret space to conduct mob business. Furthermore, in March of 1998, Harry Caray's current owners found a false wall deep in the basement, behind which was discovered a one thousand-square-foot vaulted chamber . . . big enough for a bootleg operation or whatever other nefarious activity you can imagine.

Bordelaise Sauce

This rich beef-based red wine sauce makes a terrific topping for grilled prime steaks.

6	*plus 6 tablespoons butter*
½	*cup flour*
½	*cup diced shallots*
2	*tablespoons diced garlic*
1¼	*cups sliced mushrooms*
½	*cup red wine*
1	*tablespoon A-1 sauce*
2	*tablespoons Worcestershire sauce*
1	*teaspoon chopped fresh thyme*
1	*teaspoon chopped fresh chives*
½	*teaspoon Tabasco*
4	*cups homemade beef stock (see page 95), or equivalent amount canned low-sodium beef broth*
⅓	*cup tomato purée*
	Salt and pepper

In a small sauté pan over medium heat, melt 6 tablespoons butter. Slowly whisk in the flour to create a roux that is light brown. When the mixture reaches a pasty consistency, remove it from the heat and set aside. In a large stockpot over medium heat melt the remaining 6 tablespoons butter. Sauté the shallots, garlic, and mushrooms until the shallots become translucent. Deglaze the pot with the red wine and reduce by half. Add the A-1 sauce, Worcestershire, thyme, chives, Tabasco, beef stock, and tomato purée. Simmer the mixture for 30 minutes. Increase the heat and bring the mixture to a boil. Stir in the roux a small amount at a time until the sauce has a gravy consistency. Remove from the heat and purée for 10 to 15 seconds. Salt and pepper to taste.

MAKES 6 CUPS

Homemade Chicken Stock

It seems like some trouble to make your own chicken stock when you can go to the store and buy it in a can or carton. But once you do it at home, you'll not likely go back to the ready-made stuff. There is no substitute for the vivid flavor of homemade chicken stock.

3	tablespoons olive oil
2	pounds chicken bones (backs, necks, breast plates)
2	carrots, roughly chopped
3	celery ribs, roughly chopped
1	onion, roughly chopped
1	leek, roughly chopped
2	whole cloves garlic
10	cups water

Heat the olive oil in a large stockpot over medium heat. Add the chicken bones and brown on all sides. Add the carrots, celery, onion, leeks, and garlic and sauté until the onions are translucent. Add the water and bring to a boil. Reduce the heat and simmer for 2 hours until the liquid is reduced by one-third. Strain. The stock can be frozen for later use.

MAKES 6 CUPS

Homemade Beef Stock

Although it takes little effort to make beef stock, it does require time. Make extra and freeze it, thus always having some on hand.

---

4 *pounds beef soup bones cut into large chunks*

12 *cups water*

2 *carrots, roughly chopped*

1 *celery rib, roughly chopped*

1 *onion, roughly chopped*

1 *leek, roughly chopped*

1 *bay leaf*

2 *sprigs fresh thyme*

12 *peppercorns*

1½ *teaspoons salt*

Preheat the oven to 400°F. In a shallow roasting pan, roast the bones in the oven, turning occasionally until they are browned, approximately 30 minutes. Remove the beef bones to a large stock pot and add the water, carrots, celery, onion, leek, bay leaf, thyme, peppercorns, and salt. Bring to a boil over medium-high heat, then reduce the heat and simmer partially covered for 2 hours, occasionally skimming the fat and foam from the top. Strain the stock. It can be frozen for later use.

MAKES 6 CUPS

Sun-Dried Tomato Vinaigrette

Use as a dressing for salad or a dip for vegetable crudités.

½   cup thinly julienned sun-dried tomatoes
1½ cups extra virgin olive oil
⅓   cup balsamic vinegar
2   tablespoons red wine vinegar
1½ tablespoons chopped fresh basil
½   tablespoon lemon juice
2   teaspoons chopped garlic
    Salt and pepper

In a large bowl, combine the sun-dried tomatoes, olive oil, balsamic vinegar, red wine vinegar, basil, lemon juice, and chopped garlic. Add salt and pepper to taste. Refrigerate. Mix well prior to serving.

MAKES 3 CUPS

Sweet Herb Vinaigrette

This classic dressing is given a sweet twist by the addition of honey. It is a bright-tasting vinaigrette that we like on a crisp chopped salad.

½   tablespoon dry English mustard

¼   cup sugar

2   teaspoons peeled, puréed garlic

2   tablespoons red wine vinegar

3   tablespoons white wine vinegar

1   tablespoon salt

1   tablespoon honey

2   tablespoons water

½   cup olive oil

2   cups canola oil

    Pinch of crushed red pepper

    Pinch of black pepper

    Pinch of oregano

    Pinch of basil

Combine the dry mustard, sugar, garlic purée, red wine vinegar, white wine vinegar, salt, honey, and water in a large bowl. Slowly whisk in the olive oil and salad oil until all the ingredients are blended. Season with the crushed red pepper, black pepper, oregano, and basil.

MAKES 4 CUPS

Raspberry Vinaigrette

Harry Caray was not a man to leave anything well enough alone. That same principle of augmenting, accenting, and amplifying anything that can be made better is fundamental to the spirit of his namesake restaurant. Here, for instance, oil-and-vinegar dressing is made not only with ordinary red wine vinegar, but with raspberry wine vinegar plus actual raspberries.

½ cup canola oil

½ cup raspberry wine vinegar

½ cup white sugar

1 tablespoon Dijon mustard

½ cup raspberries

3 tablespoons honey

3 tablespoons red wine vinegar

¼ teaspoon dried oregano

Combine the canola oil, raspberry vinegar, sugar, mustard, raspberries, honey, red wine vinegar, and oregano in a food processor or blender and purée. Refrigerate before using.

MAKES 3 CUPS

Harry's Caesar Dressing

Caesar dressing is customarily made in a large wooden bowl that serves as a kind of mortar for crushing the garlic and anchovies together. It is also possible to make the dressing separately and combine it with the lettuce just before serving.

½ cup egg yolks

1 cup olive oil

2 tablespoons chopped garlic

8 anchovy fillets

⅓ cup lemon juice

½ teaspoon Tabasco

1 teaspoon Worcestershire sauce

2 teaspoons Dijon mustard

⅓ cup extra virgin olive oil

   Salt and pepper

In a medium bowl, whisk together the egg yolks and olive oil. In a food processor or blender, combine the chopped garlic, anchovies, lemon juice, Tabasco, Worcestershire, mustard, and olive oil and purée. Whisk the puréed mixture into the egg yolk and olive oil mixture. Add the salt and pepper to taste.

MAKES 3 CUPS

Italian Vinaigrette

This potent dressing is a staple at Harry Caray's and is classic enough to be served as its house dressing.

2   cups olive oil

1   cup peanut oil

⅔   cup balsamic vinegar

⅔   cup red wine vinegar

¼   cup lemon juice

3   tablespoons white wine

1   teaspoon Worcestershire sauce

½   teaspoon Tabasco

1   teaspoon granulated garlic

1   teaspoon black pepper

1½   tablespoons salt

1   tablespoon oregano

½   yellow onion, scored

Whisk together the olive oil, peanut oil, balsamic vinegar, red wine vinegar, lemon juice, wine, Worcestershire, Tabasco, garlic, black pepper, salt, and oregano. Put the vinaigrette into a plastic container and add the onion. Cover and refrigerate overnight. Remove the onion and the vinaigrette is ready to serve.

MAKES 5 CUPS

• PASTA •
& RISOTTO

Rigatoni with Vodka Sauce

Rotini with Italian Sausage

Linguine Carbonara

Fettuccini Alfredo Primavera

Baked Ziti

Ziti with Grilled Chicken and Pesto Sauce

Meat Lasagna

Spaghetti with Italian Meatballs

Pasta with Aglio Olio Sauce

Linguine di Mare

Shrimp Scampi over Capellini

Linguine with White Clam Sauce

Linguine with Red Clam Sauce

Linguine with Lemon-Garlic Shrimp

Basic Risotto

Sweet Potato and Wild Mushroom Risotto

Grilled Halibut Fillet with Chanterelle Risotto

Saffron Risotto with Grilled Sea Scallops

Filet Mignon Served over Barolo Risotto

Roasted Vegetable Risotto

Risotto with Oven-Roasted Chicken

Risotto with Pancetta, Arugula, and Goat Cheese

Risotto with Italian Sausage and Leeks

Rigatoni with Vodka Sauce

There is a world of difference between pre-grated Parmesan cheese and a nice chunk of Parmigiano-Reggiano that gets freshly shaved to garnish a plate of pasta. This rigatoni demands shavings of the "King of All Grating Cheeses" to help accentuate its plush flavors. And here, as in most other pastas, it is crucial to cook the noodles *al dente*, which literally means "to the teeth"—tender, but still slightly chewy. Pasta that retains a certain firmness always brings character to a dish.

1	*pound rigatoni, cooked al dente*
¼	*cup olive oil*
4	*Roma tomatoes, diced*
3	*shallots, diced*
6	*cloves fresh garlic, finely chopped*
¼	*cup chopped fresh basil leaves*
½	*cup vodka*
1	*cup alfredo sauce (see page 83)*
2	*cups marinara sauce (see page 81)*
½	*cup mascarpone cheese*
½	*cup shaved Parmigiano-Reggiano cheese*
	Salt and pepper

Heat a large sauté pan over medium heat. Once the pan is hot, add the olive oil, tomatoes, shallots, garlic, and basil. Sauté until the shallots are translucent and the garlic is lightly browned. Remove from heat and deglaze the pan with the vodka. Simmer until reduced by one-quarter and add the alfredo sauce, marinara sauce, and mascarpone cheese. Bring the mixture to a simmer and toss with the rigatoni. Add the Parmigiano-Reggiano immediately prior to serving. Salt and pepper to taste.

MAKES 4 SERVINGS

Rotini with Italian Sausage, Fennel, and Portobello Mushrooms

Rotini look like little springs. They are an especially good pasta shape with chunky sauces. The longer version of rotini, fusilli, can be substituted. Ricotta salata is an especially good garnish for this dish because of its nutty sweet flavor—a great complement to the spicy sausage and earthy mushrooms.

---

1   *cup roasted portobello mushroom caps (about 4 caps)*
    Salt and pepper
    Olive oil
1   *cup fennel bulbs*
1   *pound uncooked spicy Italian sausage*
3   *cups rotini pasta, cooked al dente*
3   *cups meat sauce (see page 82)*
½   *cup shredded ricotta salata cheese*

Preheat the oven to 400°F. To prepare the portobello mushroom caps, scrape off the gills, or dark underside. Season the mushroom caps with the salt and pepper and then sprinkle them with olive oil. Place the mushrooms on a cookie sheet and bake in the oven for approximately 5 minutes or until the mushrooms are cooked through. To prepare the fennel, cut away the bottom ½ inch of the bulb. Slice the bulbs lengthwise into ½-inch slices. Season the fennel with salt and pepper and sprinkle it with olive oil. Grill on a grill, or broil in the oven for 6 or 7 minutes, turning at least twice, until the fennel becomes translucent. To prepare the Italian sausage, brown each side under the broiler and then turn the oven to bake at 400°F. Bake the sausage for 8 to 10 minutes or to an internal temperature of 145°F. Cut the portobello mushrooms and the fennel into ¾-inch squares. Cut the sausage into ½-inch, bias-cut slices. In a large saucepan over medium heat, combine the meat sauce, mushrooms, fennel, and sausage. Bring the mixture to a simmer and then toss it with the cooked rotini. Put on a large serving platter or pasta bowl and garnish with the shredded ricotta salata cheese.

MAKES 4 TO 6 SERVINGS

Linguine Carbonara

Carbonara is a Roman way of saucing pasta, always including pancetta, eggs, and Parmigiano-Reggiano cheese. Harry Caray's version heightens its richness with the addition of Alfredo sauce.

2   *cups water*

⅔   *cup frozen green peas*

⅓   *pound pancetta, thinly sliced and diced*

½   *pound button mushrooms, cleaned and sliced*

3   *cups alfredo sauce (see page 83)*

2   *eggs*

½   *cup Parmigiano-Reggiano cheese*

1   *pound linguine, cooked al dente*

4   *to 6 sprigs parsley*

Put the water in a medium saucepan over high heat and bring to a boil. Drop the peas in the boiling water for 1 minute and immediately strain off the liquid and rinse with cold water. In a small sauté pan over medium heat, sauté the pancetta until it browns. Strain the oil off of the pancetta, reserving 1 tablespoon. Put the reserved oil into a medium sauté pan over medium flame. Add the mushrooms and sauté until soft. In a medium stockpot, combine the alfredo sauce, eggs, Parmigiana-Reggiano, pancetta, mushrooms, and green peas. Heat the mixture over medium heat and stir until all the ingredients are thoroughly combined. Toss the sauce with the cooked linguine. Serve the pasta immediately in four to six individual bowls. Garnish each bowl with a parsley sprig.

MAKES 4 TO 6 SERVINGS

Fettuccini Alfredo Primavera

First served in 1914 in a Roman restaurant owned by Alfredo Di Lello, fettuccini Alfredo was "discovered" by Hollywood movie stars Mary Pickford and Douglas Fairbanks while they were honeymooning in Italy in the late 1920s. The original recipe they brought back to the U.S. contained no cream, just lots of butter and cheese.

8   cups water
⅓   cup broccoli florets
⅓   cup cauliflower florets
⅓   cup diced onion
¼   cup diced green pepper
¼   cup diced red pepper
¼   cup diced yellow pepper
⅓   cup frozen or fresh green beans
⅓   cup diced zucchini
⅓   cup diced yellow squash
4   cups alfredo sauce (see page 83)
1   tablespoon fresh chopped parsley
1½ pounds fettuccini, cooked al dente
1   cup freshly grated Parmigiano-Reggiano cheese, optional

Bring the water to a boil in a large stockpot over high heat. Add the broccoli and cauliflower and boil for 1 minute. Add the onion, green pepper, red pepper, yellow pepper, green beans, zucchini, and yellow squash. Boil the vegetables until the onion becomes translucent and the rest of the vegetables soften. Strain the water out of the pot and add the alfredo sauce and parsley. Cook over medium heat until the sauce is heated through. Toss the sauce with the cooked fettuccini and serve immediately. Offer the freshly grated Parmigiano-Reggiano.

MAKES 6 TO 8 SERVINGS

Baked Ziti

The long, thin macaroni tubes known as ziti lend themselves especially well to baked casseroles. In this classic version of the dish, the traditional duo of pasta and tomato is brought together with plenty of mozzarella cheese that turns molten and makes each forkful an adventure in twirling.

---

2   *tablespoons olive oil*

2   *garlic cloves, minced*

1   *(28-ounce) can crushed tomatoes*

2   *tablespoons chopped fresh basil*

     Salt

1   *pound ziti, cooked al dente*

½   *pound mozzarella cheese, shredded*

¼   *cup grated Parmesan cheese*

Preheat the oven to 400°F. In a medium saucepan, heat the olive oil over medium heat. Sauté the garlic until it is soft, about 2 minutes. Add the tomatoes, basil, and salt to taste and simmer until the sauce becomes thick, 8 to 10 minutes. In a large bowl combine the pasta and the tomato sauce. Grease a baking dish and pour half of the pasta mixture into the dish. Sprinkle with half of the mozzarella and half of the Parmesan cheese. Pour the remaining pasta on top and sprinkle with the remaining mozzarella and Parmesan cheeses. Bake for 20 minutes or until the cheese is bubbling and golden. Let it rest for 5 to 7 minutes before serving.

MAKES 4 TO 6 SERVINGS

Ziti with Grilled Chicken and Pesto Sauce

A brilliant-flavored, hearty meal, in this ziti dish it is vital to use good-quality pasta and to cook it al dente. If too soft, the noodles will be lost among the other power-hitting ingredients.

3 *(7-ounce) skinless, boneless chicken breasts, seasoned and grilled*

½ *cup olive oil*

⅔ *cup sun-dried tomatoes*

½ *cup porcini mushrooms*

2 *zucchini, cleaned and sliced into ¼-inch rounds*

⅔ *cup pitted kalamata olives*

1 *cup pesto sauce (see page 85)*

¾ *cup homemade chicken stock (see page 94),*
   or equivalent amount canned low-sodium chicken broth

1 *pound ziti, cooked al dente*

1 *cup freshly grated Parmigiano-Reggiano cheese, optional*

Dice the grilled chicken breasts into ¾-inch cubes. Heat the olive oil in a large stockpot over high heat. Add the tomatoes, mushrooms, chicken, zucchini, and olives. Sauté until the zucchini softens. Add the pesto sauce and the chicken stock. Bring the mixture to a boil and stir until thoroughly combined. Toss with the cooked ziti and serve immediately. Offer the freshly grated Parmigiano-Reggiano.

MAKES 4 TO 6 SERVINGS

Meat Lasagna

The quintessential Italian casserole is a dish that Americans have come to love, not only for its comfort-food taste, but for its convenience. Lasagna travels well, and it can be made ahead and served later, making it ideal for potluck suppers.

1½   pounds ground beef
⅓   cup olive oil
     Pinch of dry oregano
     Pinch of dry basil
     Salt and pepper
1   cup grated Romano cheese
1   cup grated Parmesan cheese
1½   pounds ricotta cheese, drained overnight
3   egg yolks
½   tablespoon chopped parsley
½   teaspoon white pepper
20   thin slices mozzarella cheese (approximately 2 pounds)
5   cups meat sauce (see page 82)
2   pounds lasagna noodles, cooked al dente

In a large sauté pan, brown the ground beef in the olive oil over medium heat. Season the mixture with the oregano, basil, and salt and pepper to taste. Strain away the excess oil and set aside. In a small bowl, mix the Romano cheese and the Parmesan cheese together and set aside. In a large mixing bowl, combine the drained ricotta cheese, egg yolks, parsley, white pepper, and ½ cup of the Romano Parmesan mixture. In a large casserole dish build 3 layers in the following order from the bottom: meat sauce, lasagna noodles, ricotta mixture, ground beef, Romano Parmesan mixture, and sliced mozzarella. Top the lasagna with a layer of meat sauce. Cover with foil and bake for 45 minutes. Remove foil, add one additional layer of mozzarella cheese and bake for an additional 10 minutes. Allow the lasagna to settle for 10 minutes before serving.

MAKES 6 TO 8 SERVINGS

Spaghetti with Italian Meatballs

There was a time, before pizza got popular, that spaghetti and meatballs virtually defined Italian cuisine in this country. As served in Italy, meatballs tend to be small, marble-sized; we Americans like them bigger.

---

3   cups meat sauce (see page 82) or marinara sauce (see page 81)

8   cups water

8   meatballs (see page 69)

1   pound spaghetti, cooked al dente

4   parsley sprigs

½   cup freshly grated Parmigiano-Reggiano cheese, optional

In a large saucepan, heat the meat sauce over a medium flame. At the same time, combine the water and meatballs in a large stockpot over high heat and bring to a boil. Strain off the water. Toss half of the meat sauce with the cooked spaghetti. Serve in 4 individual bowls. Top each bowl of pasta with 2 meatballs and ladle the remaining sauce on top of the meatballs. Garnish each bowl with a parsley sprig and serve immediately. Offer freshly grated Parmigiano-Reggiano cheese.

MAKES 4 SERVINGS

Pasta with Aglio Olio Sauce (Garlic and Olive Oil)

Nothing's simpler or easier to prepare than pasta aglio olio. Made with only the best extra virgin olive oil and plenty of fresh garlic, dressed with just-grated Parmigiano-Reggiano, it may well be a perfect dish!

---

6   tablespoons extra virgin olive oil

¼   cup minced garlic

4   tablespoons chopped fresh parsley

2   teaspoons lemon juice

1   pound pasta, cooked al dente,
     reserving ½ cup of the cooking water

     Pinch of red pepper flakes

½   cup freshly grated Parmigiano-Reggiano cheese

     Freshly ground black pepper

     Salt

In a large sauté pan, heat the olive oil over medium heat. Add the garlic and sauté until the garlic becomes golden, but not browned. Add the parsley and the lemon juice. Toss in the pasta and the pepper flakes. Slowly add the reserved cooking water and sauté for an additional minute. Serve in individual bowls and top with the Parmigiano-Reggiano and black pepper and salt to taste.

MAKES 4 SERVINGS

Linguine di Mare

While other kinds of pasta can be used in this dish, linguine is just right to use as a kind of edible net to help twirl pieces of seafood up onto a fork. Don't overcook the seafood, lest it toughen.

---

2   cups chopped sea clams

2   dozen fresh littleneck clams

2   dozen fresh black mussels

1   pound cleaned and sliced squid

1   pound cleaned and sliced polpo (baby octopuses)

12   headless (size U12) shrimp, peeled, deveined, and butterflied

2   cups clam juice

2   tablespoons chopped parsley

1   teaspoon oregano

1   tablespoon chopped fresh garlic

¼   cup olive oil

½   cup white wine

¾   cup marinara sauce (see page 81)

    Salt and white pepper

2   pounds linguine, cooked al dente

6   to 8 sprigs parsley

In a large stockpot, combine the sea clams, littleneck clams, mussels, squid, polpo, shrimp, clam juice, parsley, oregano, garlic, olive oil, white wine, and the marinara sauce. Simmer the mixture, covered, over medium heat until the littleneck clams and the mussels open. Salt and pepper the mixture to taste. In a large serving bowl, toss the linguini with half of the clam liquid from the stockpot. Remove the littleneck clams and the mussels from the stockpot and arrange them around the outside of the dish. Pour the remaining clam liquid with the clams, squid, polpo, and shrimp over the top of the pasta. Garnish the bowl with the parsley sprigs and serve immediately.

MAKES 6 TO 8 SERVINGS

Shrimp Scampi over Capellini

Scampi is from the Venetian word for prawn, but in the U.S. it has come to mean a luxurious garlicky sauce customarily used to envelop shrimp.

---

16 *headless (size U12) shrimp, peeled, deveined, and butterflied*
    Flour
¼   *cup olive oil*
½   *cup butter*
1½ *tablespoons chopped garlic*
1½ *cups homemade chicken stock (see page 94),*
    or equivalent amount canned low-sodium chicken broth
1   *tablespoon chopped parsley*
    Salt and white pepper
1   *pound capellini, cooked al dente*
4   *parsley sprigs*
1   *cup freshly grated Parmigiano-Reggiano cheese, optional*

Dredge each shrimp in the flour. Heat the olive oil in a large sauté pan over high heat. Slowly add the shrimp and cook until opaque, 2 to 3 minutes. Remove the shrimp and set aside. Add the butter and garlic and sauté until the garlic browns, 1 to 2 minutes. Add the chicken stock and parsley and season with the salt and white pepper to taste. Simmer for 2 to 3 minutes. Toss the capellini with half of the sauce from the pan, and serve in four individual pasta bowls. Return the shrimp to the sauté pan for 30 seconds. Pour the remaining sauce over the top of the pasta and top each bowl with 4 shrimp. Garnish each bowl with a parsley sprig. Offer freshly grated Parmigiano-Reggiano cheese.

MAKES 4 SERVINGS

Linguine with White Clam Sauce

The flavor and aroma of fresh, sweet littlenecks with garlic and wine are fundamental pleasures of southern Italian cooking.

---

2   cups chopped sea clams
2   dozen fresh littleneck clams
2   cups clam juice
2   tablespoons chopped parsley
1   teaspoon oregano
1   tablespoon chopped fresh garlic
½   cup olive oil
¾   cup white wine
    Salt and white pepper
1½ pounds linguine, cooked al dente
6   sprigs parsley

In a large stockpot, combine the sea clams, littleneck clams, clam juice, parsley, oregano, chopped garlic, olive oil, and white wine. Simmer the mixture, covered, over medium heat until the littleneck clams open. Salt and pepper the mixture to taste. In a large serving bowl, toss the linguini with half of the clam liquid from the stockpot. Remove the littleneck clams from the stockpot and arrange them around the outside of the dish. Pour the remaining clam liquid over the top of the pasta. Garnish the bowl with the parsley sprigs and serve immediately.

MAKES 6 SERVINGS

Harry Caray has always been larger than life.

Harry Caray's restaurant is located in one of Chicago's most architecturally significant buildings. It received landmark status in 2001.

There's plenty of elbow room at Harry Caray's, where you dine off thick white linen amidst a storehouse of baseball memorabilia.

Harry Caray at his bar with his beloved staff . . . and beloved beverage.

Some of Harry Caray's favorite things: steak, chicken Vesuvio, plenty of wine, and a life devoted to baseball.

The Wrigley Room, one of the rooms on the second floor that is used for private parties. On the left is a credenza from the original Arlington Park racetrack.

No restaurant has better munchies. Here, just in front of a Harry Caray-faced baseball, set on a vintage seat from the White Sox's old Comiskey Park, is a plate of fried calamari. The best place to do your munching is in the barroom (below), where Holy Cow! potato chips are set all along the bar's sixty-foot, six-inch length.

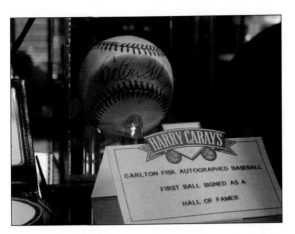

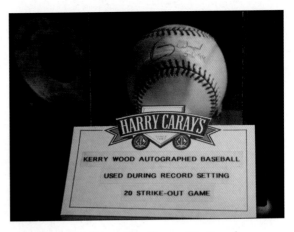

Carlton Fisk was a right-handed catcher who spent an amazing 24 years behind the plate and was an eleven-time All-Star. He played for the Boston Red Sox and the Chicago White Sox.

Cubs pitcher Kerry Wood was National League Rookie of the Year in 1998, when he struck out an amazing 20 players in one game, then 13 in his next. Thirty-three strikeouts in two consecutive games is a Major League record.

An actual "Holy Cow", wearing Harry Caray's trademark glasses, stands in the restaurant hallway. It was created in 1999 for a Chicago art event called "Cows on Parade."

Dutchie and Harry Caray at home plate in Wrigley Field.

Dutchie Caray shares a table with Harry "Chip" Caray III, Harry's grandson and current announcer for the Chicago Cubs.

Roast beef is sliced to order at the sandwich cart in the barroom.

Executive chef Garrick Dickie

**Prime Rib Sandwich
Au Jus**

**Harry's
Bruschetta
(page 49)**

**Pan-Seared,
Peppered
Yellowfin
Tuna with
Pinot Grigio
Butter Sauce
(page 137)**

**Chicken
Picatta
(page 158)**

**Jumbo Lump
Crab Cakes
(page 52)**

**Harry's
Signature
New York
Strip, Pepper-
corn Style
(page 163)**

**Linguine di Mare
(page 112)**

**Lamb
Chops
Oreganato
(page 176)**

**Surf and Turf
(page 181)**

**Linguine
with White
Clam Sauce
(page 114)**

**Baked Clams
(page 55)**

**Plum-Glazed
Salmon with
Polenta and Fried
Leeks (page 142)**

Harry's Signature Chicken Vesuvio (page 149)

Veal Parmigiana (page 169)

**Crème Brûlée
(page 194)**

**Chocolate
Torta with
Warm Caramel
Pecan Sauce
(page 192)**

Linguine with Red Clam Sauce

Quick and easy to make, healthy and delicious, linguine with tomato-based clam sauce is popular in Italian restaurants all across America.

2   cups chopped sea clams
2   dozen fresh littleneck clams
1   cup clam juice
2   tablespoons chopped parsley
1   teaspoon oregano
1   tablespoon fresh chopped garlic
¼   cup olive oil
½   cup white wine
¾   cup marinara sauce (see page 81)
    Salt and white pepper
1½ pounds linguine, cooked al dente
6   sprigs parsley

In a large stockpot, combine the sea clams, littleneck clams, clam juice, parsley, oregano, garlic, olive oil, white wine, and marinara sauce. Simmer the mixture, covered, over medium heat until the littleneck clams open. Salt and pepper to taste. In a large serving bowl, toss the warm linguine with half of the red sauce from the stockpot. Remove the littleneck clams from the stockpot and arrange them around the outside of the dish. Pour the remaining red sauce over the top of the pasta. Garnish the bowl with the parsley sprigs and serve immediately.

MAKES 6 SERVINGS

Linguine with Lemon-Garlic Shrimp and Parmigiano-Reggiano Cream Sauce

A celebration meal that demands the biggest and best shrimp you can find. The Parmigiano-Reggiano cream sauce may require a couple of pieces of bread. You'll want to mop every drop of it from the plate.

FOR THE MARINADE:

¼   *cup extra virgin olive oil*

¼   *cup lemon juice*

3   *garlic cloves, finely diced*

1   *teaspoon finely diced lemon zest*

24 *headless (size U12) shrimp, peeled, deveined, and butterflied*

FOR THE CREAM SAUCE:

2   *cups white wine*

2   *shallots, minced*

2   *cups homemade chicken stock (page 94),*
    or equivalent amount canned low-sodium chicken broth

2   *cups heavy cream*

⅔   *cup grated Parmigiano-Reggiano cheese*
    Salt and white pepper

TO ASSEMBLE THE DISH:

1   *pound green beans*
    Salt and pepper

2   *pounds linguine, cooked al dente*

6   *lemon wheels*

1   *tablespoon chopped parsley*

Combine the olive oil, lemon juice, garlic, and lemon zest in a small bowl. Put the shrimp in a shallow baking dish, cover them with the olive oil mixture, and refrigerate for a minimum of 1 hour.

To make the cream sauce, combine the white wine and shallots in a large saucepan, and cook over high heat until reduced by three-quarters. Add the chicken stock and continue cooking until the mixture is reduced by half. Add the cream and continue to cook over high heat. Add the Parmigiano-Reggiano and season with the salt and white pepper to taste.

To assemble the dish, blanch the green beans by placing them in boiling water for 1 minute and then rinsing them with cold water. Put 3 tablespoons of the shrimp marinade in a large sauté pan over medium heat. Add the shrimp and sauté until the shrimp become opaque all the way through. Add the blanched green beans and sauté until they are heated through. Add the salt and pepper to taste. Toss the cooked linguine with the cream sauce and transfer to six individual plates or bowls. Evenly divide the shrimp and the green beans and place them on top of each plate of pasta. Garnish each plate with a lemon wheel and the chopped parsley.

MAKES 6 SERVINGS

Basic Risotto

Risotto was virtually unknown in America until a few decades ago, but it has become one of the most popular items on fine Italian restaurant menus. It is made with Arborio rice (a short, fat-grained Italian rice), and it differs from ordinary rice in that it is always slow-cooked with flavored broth (and sometimes other ingredients) until it attains a thick, creamy consistency and the rice is saturated with the flavors of its cooking media.

---

2   tablespoons olive oil

2   tablespoons unsalted butter

1   medium yellow onion, diced

4   cups Arborio rice

6   cups homemade chicken stock (see page 94),
    or equivalent amount canned low-sodium chicken broth

In a heavy-bottomed saucepan, heat the olive oil and the butter. Sauté the onions over medium heat until they become clear. Add the rice and stir for 1 minute. Add enough chicken stock to cover the rice and stir. Bring the mixture to a boil and then reduce the heat to a simmer. Add the rest of the chicken stock, ½ cup at a time, stirring continually, as the mixture reduces. Total approximate cooking time is 20 minutes.

MAKES 4 TO 6 SERVINGS

Sweet Potato
and Wild Mushroom Risotto

A deeply satisfying, earthy risotto that tastes especially good on cold autumn nights.

1	large sweet potato, baked and peeled
2	cups balsamic vinegar
1	tablespoon butter
1	tablespoon olive oil
½	pound chanterelle mushrooms
½	pound shiitake mushrooms, sliced and stemmed
½	cup white wine
6	cups basic risotto (see page 118)
½	cup grated Asiago cheese
2	tablespoons toasted pine nuts
½	tablespoon chopped parsley

Purée the sweet potato in a blender or food processor. In a saucepan, simmer the balsamic vinegar until it reduces to ¼ cup. Heat the butter and the olive oil in a large sauté pan. Add the mushrooms and sauté until the mushrooms are soft. Deglaze the pan with the white wine. Add the risotto and stir. Add the sweet potato purée and stir until the mixture is thoroughly combined. Toss the mixture with the cheese. Serve on individual plates by mounding the risotto in the center of the plate. Sprinkle with the toasted pine nuts and chopped parsley.

MAKES 4 TO 6 SERVINGS

Grilled Halibut Fillet with Broccoli and Chanterelle Mushroom Risotto

While risotto is frequently a meal unto itself, it also does a great job of supporting meat or fish. In this case it is the foundation for a meal of grilled halibut fillets.

For the halibut:

2	*tablespoons olive oil*
½	*tablespoon chopped rosemary*
½	*tablespoon chopped sage*
4	*(8-ounce) fresh halibut fillets*

For the risotto:

2	*tablespoons olive oil*
2	*tablespoons butter*
1	*cup broccoli florets*
1	*cup sliced chanterelle mushrooms*
½	*cup pitted and sliced black olives*
1	*cup diced Roma tomatoes*

2	*tablespoons garlic purée*
1	*tablespoon chopped garlic*
½	*tablespoon chopped rosemary*
½	*tablespoon chopped sage*
¼	*cup white wine*
½	*cup homemade chicken stock (page 94), or equivalent amount canned low-sodium chicken broth*
6	*cups basic risotto (see page 118)*
¾	*cup grated fontina cheese*
	Salt and black pepper
4	*sprigs parsley*

Combine the olive oil, rosemary, and sage in a small mixing bowl. Rub the oil mixture on each of the fillets and refrigerate.

Heat the olive oil and butter in a large sauté pan over medium heat. Add the broccoli, mushrooms, olives, tomatoes, garlic purée, chopped garlic, rosemary, and sage. Sauté the mixture until the vegetables become tender. Deglaze the pan with the white wine. Simmer the mixture until it reduces by half. Add the chicken stock and bring the mixture to a boil. Add the risotto and stir until smooth and creamy. Add the fontina cheese and salt and black pepper to taste.

To assemble the dish, grill the marinated halibut fillets for 3 minutes on each side, or until the fillets are cooked through. Do not overcook the fish. Place a mound of risotto in the center of each of four individual plates. Place a halibut fillet on top of the risotto and garnish each plate with a parsley sprig and serve.

MAKES 4 SERVINGS

Saffron Risotto with Cremini Mushrooms, Asparagus, and Grilled Sea Scallops

Saffron risotto is said to have been invented in the fifteenth century by an artist called Valerio of Flanders. With his sense of color heightened by his work on a series of stained glass windows, Valerio got the idea to tint his risotto a sunny yellow by the use of saffron.

2	plus 2 tablespoons plus 1 tablespoon olive oil	16	(10- to 20-count) sea scallops
2	tablespoons plus 1 tablespoon butter		Pinch of salt
1	medium yellow onion, diced		Pinch of granulated garlic
½	teaspoon saffron		Pinch of white pepper
4	cups Arborio rice	16	asparagus spears, cleaned, trimmed, and blanched
6	cups homemade chicken stock (see page 94), or equivalent amount canned low-salt chicken broth	½	pound cremini mushrooms, cleaned and sliced
		⅓	cup heavy cream
		¼	cup grated Parmigiano-Reggiano cheese
		4	to 6 parsley sprigs

Heat 2 tablespoons olive oil and 2 tablespoons butter in a medium-size, heavy-bottomed saucepan. Sauté the onion and saffron until the onion becomes translucent. Add the rice and stir for 1 minute. Add enough chicken stock to cover the rice and stir. Bring the mixture to a boil and then reduce the heat to a simmer. Add the rest of the chicken stock, ½ cup at a time, stirring continually, as the mixture reduces. Total approximate cooking time is 20 minutes.

Season the sea scallops with 1 tablespoon olive oil, salt, garlic, and pepper. Grill the scallops for 2 minutes on each side or until they are cooked through. Slice the asparagus spears on a bias into ½-inch pieces. Heat the remaining 2 tablespoons olive oil and the remaining butter in a large sauté pan. Sauté the asparagus and the mushrooms until the mushrooms become soft. Add the risotto, heavy cream, and Parmigiano-Reggiano cheese to the scallops and vegetables. Simmer for 2 minutes or until the risotto thickens. Add salt and white pepper to taste. Mound the risotto on four to six individual plates and place the sea scallops on top of the risotto. Garnish with the parsley sprigs and serve.

MAKES 4 TO 6 SERVINGS

Filet Mignon Served over Barolo Risotto with Parmesan Crisps

A *basso profundo* meal that will take care of the most powerful cravings for meat and potatoes. Prime beef and red wine with character are essential.

6	large asparagus stalks, trimmed	1	tablespoon chopped fresh basil
1	cup freshly grated Parmigiano-Reggiano cheese	1	teaspoon chopped fresh rosemary
		2	teaspoons chopped garlic
6	(6-ounce) prime filet mignons	6	cups basic risotto (see page 118)
	Lawry's seasoned salt	1	cup Barolo wine (may substitute another full-bodied red wine)
	Black pepper		
2	tablespoons butter	1	cup heavy cream
⅓	cup diced shallots	6	parsley sprigs

Preheat the oven to 350°F. Blanch the asparagus by placing it in boiling water for 2 to 3 minutes, and then rinsing it in cold water. Dice the stalks into ½-inch pieces and set aside. Working on a nonstick baking mat or parchment paper on a cookie sheet, take a cookie cutter (3 inches in diameter) and fill it ½ inch thick with the Parmigiano-Reggiano cheese. Repeat 5 times until you have six rounds. Bake in the oven until they begin to bubble and turn brown. Remove the crisps from the oven and allow them to cool. Season the filets with the Lawry's and the pepper. Mark the filets on the grill or broil in the oven on each side for 1 minute. Transfer the filets to the oven and bake them until they reach the desired temperature. In a large sauté pan, heat the butter over medium heat. Sauté the shallots with the basil, rosemary, and garlic until they become translucent. Stir in the risotto, asparagus, red wine, and heavy cream and simmer the mixture until the liquid reduces and the risotto thickens. To serve, mound the risotto in the center of individual plates. Lean the filet against the risotto and carefully press the edge of the Parmesan crisp into the top of the risotto. Garnish each plate with a parsley sprig and serve.

MAKES 6 SERVINGS

Roasted Vegetable Risotto

From artichokes to tomatoes to zucchini, vegetables play a huge role in Italian cooking. Feel free to substitute or add other roasted vegetables to this meatless but endlessly hearty risotto.

1½ red bell peppers, seeded and cut into ½-inch pieces	Black pepper
1 large eggplant, peeled and cut into ½-inch pieces	1 tablespoon butter
1½ zucchini, cut into ½-inch pieces	½ pound button mushrooms, quartered
2 carrots, cut into ½-inch pieces	¼ teaspoon crushed red pepper flakes
2 tablespoons chopped garlic	¼ cup white wine
6 plum tomatoes, quartered	¾ cup homemade chicken stock (see page 94), or equivalent amount canned low-sodium chicken broth
¼ teaspoon thyme	
¼ teaspoon basil	6 cups basic risotto (see page 118)
¼ teaspoon oregano	1 tablespoon balsamic vinegar
3 plus 1 tablespoons olive oil	1 cup Pecorino Romano cheese
Salt	2 tablespoons chopped parsley
	2 tablespoons julienned fresh basil

To roast the vegetables, preheat the oven to 450°F. In a large mixing bowl, toss the peppers, eggplant, zucchini, carrots, garlic, tomatoes, thyme, basil, and oregano with the 3 tablespoons olive oil. Season with the salt and black pepper to taste. Transfer the vegetables to a roasting pan and roast them in the oven for 20 to 25 minutes, or until they are tender, stirring occasionally.

In a large sauté pan, heat the butter and the remaining olive oil over medium heat. Add the mushrooms and sauté until they are soft. Add the crushed red pepper flakes. Deglaze the pan with the white wine and reduce the liquid by one-quarter. Add the chicken stock, risotto, roasted vegetables, vinegar, Pecorino Romano, parsley, and basil. Simmer until the risotto thickens.

MAKES 4 TO 6 SERVINGS

Risotto with Oven-Roasted Chicken, Caramelized Onions, and Portobello Mushrooms

Just when you thought that risotto couldn't get any more luxurious, you cook this recipe with its creamy infusion of cheeses and find a whole new level of Arborio satisfaction.

4	(7-ounce) boneless, skinless chicken breasts	2	cups heavy whipping cream
1	tablespoon olive oil	2	cups homemade chicken stock (see page 94), or equivalent amount canned low-sodium chicken broth
2	tablespoons mixed fresh herbs (basil, rosemary, thyme)	½	cup grated Pecorino Romano cheese
4	tablespoons butter	½	cup grated Gruyère cheese (may substitute Swiss cheese)
2	large yellow onions, thinly sliced		
1	pound portobello mushrooms, stemmed, gills removed, and thinly sliced	2	tablespoons chopped parsley
		¼	cup julianned fresh basil
2	tablespoons chopped garlic		Salt and white pepper
6	cups basic risotto (see page 118)		

Preheat the oven to 400°F. Coat the chicken breasts with the olive oil and rub the mixed fresh herbs on each breast. Place the seasoned chicken in a roasting pan and roast for 20 minutes or until the chicken is cooked through. Remove the chicken from the oven, allow to cool, and dice into ¾-inch pieces. In a large sauté pan, melt the butter over medium heat. Add the onions and sauté until they begin to brown (caramelize). Add the mushrooms and garlic and sauté until the mushrooms become soft. Add the risotto, whipping cream, chicken stock, Pecorino Romano, and Gruyère. Simmer together until the risotto thickens. Add the parsley, basil, and salt and pepper to taste, toss, and serve.

MAKES 4 TO 6 SERVINGS

Risotto with Pancetta, Arugula, and Goat Cheese

One of our basic rules of cooking is that everything (except dessert) tastes better with bacon. Here is a risotto laced with pancetta, the salty smack of which makes it an inspired companion for peppery-flavored arugula and smooth cheeses.

1	plus 1 tablespoon olive oil	6	cups basic risotto (see page 118)
1	tablespoon chopped garlic	2	tablespoons balsamic vinegar
¼	teaspoon crushed red pepper flakes	¾	cup grated Parmigiano-Reggiano cheese
½	pound arugula, coarsely chopped	¾	cup crumbled goat cheese
	Salt	1½	cups homemade chicken stock (see page 94), or equivalent amount canned low-sodium chicken broth
	Black pepper		
½	cup thinly sliced and diced pancetta	¼	cup chopped parsley
1	large yellow onion, chopped	1	tablespoon finely chopped fresh rosemary
2	cups stemmed and halved cherry tomatoes		

Heat 1 tablespoon olive oil in a large sauté pan over medium heat. Add the garlic and red pepper flakes. Sauté until the garlic begins to brown. Add the arugula and cover. Sauté for 2 minutes. Remove the cover and season the arugula with salt and pepper to taste. Heat the remaining 1 tablespoon olive oil in a large saucepan over medium-high heat. Add the pancetta and sauté until crispy. Add the onion and sauté until it becomes translucent. Strain off the excess oil. Add the tomatoes, risotto, vinegar, Parmigiano-Reggiano, goat cheese, and chicken stock. Simmer until the risotto thickens. Toss in the arugula, parsley, and rosemary and serve immediately.

MAKES 4 TO 6 SERVINGS

Risotto with Italian Sausage and Leeks

While this recipe calls for mild Italian sausage, the sweetness of which balances well with the leek, it also works with hot, spicy sausage.

2   *tablespoons olive oil*

2   *tablespoons butter*

1   *leek bulb, minced*

⅔   *pound mild Italian sausage, skinned and crumbled*

6   *cups basic risotto (see page 118)*

1   *cup homemade chicken stock (see page 94),*
     or equivalent amount canned low-sodium chicken broth

½   *cup heavy whipping cream*

1   *cup freshly grated Parmigiano-Reggiano cheese*
     Salt
     White pepper

1   *tablespoon chopped chives*

Heat the olive oil and butter in a large saucepan over medium heat. Add the leeks and sauté until they become translucent. Add the sausage and sauté until browned, approximately 10 minutes. Remove the sausage and leeks from the pan, reserving the olive oil and butter. Add the risotto, chicken stock, whipping cream, and cheese to the saucepan and simmer until the risotto thickens. Add the sausage and leek and season with the salt and pepper to taste. Garnish with the chives.

MAKES 4 TO 6 SERVINGS

· ITALIAN · FAVORITES

Italian Sausage and Peppers

Eggplant Parmigiana

Marco Polo

Osso Buco

*Homemade Gnocchi
with Roasted Red Peppers and Mushrooms*

Stuffed Sweet Red Peppers

Italian Sausage and Peppers

A prototypical southern Italian combination, now beloved throughout America. Quality of sausage makes all the difference in this dish. Fresh-made from an Italian butcher is the way to go.

---

4 pounds Italian sausage

½ cup olive oil

2 large red peppers, seeded and sliced into 6 strips

2 large green peppers, seeded and sliced into 6 strips

2 large yellow peppers, seeded and sliced into 6 strips

1 teaspoon oregano

1 teaspoon salt

½ teaspoon black pepper

1½ teaspoons granulated garlic

1 tablespoon chopped parsley

1 cup white wine

1½ cups homemade chicken stock (page 94),
   or equivalent amount canned low-sodium chicken broth

Preheat the oven to 400°F. Slice the Italian sausage into 24 even pieces (approximately 3-inch pieces). Place the sausage on an ungreased cookie sheet and bake for 15 to 20 minutes, turning the sausages during baking so they brown on all sides. Remove the sausages from the oven and set aside. In a large sauté pan, heat the olive oil over medium heat and sauté the peppers until they soften. Add the sausages to the sauté pan and season the mixture with the oregano, salt, black pepper, garlic, and chopped parsley. Deglaze the pan with the white wine and reduce by half. Add the chicken stock. Transfer the sausage and peppers to a baking dish and bake in the oven for 10 minutes. Arrange the sausages in a spoke pattern in the center of 6 to 8 plates, depending on serving size. On each plate, arrange two slices of red pepper, two slices of green pepper, and two slices of yellow pepper over the sausages. Pour the pan juices over the sausage and peppers and serve immediately.

MAKES 6 TO 8 SERVINGS

Eggplant Parmigiana

Eggplant parmigiana is an Italian-sounding food that is in fact American in origin. Made with Harry Caray's hearty meat sauce, it is a grand meal.

3   *large eggplants, peeled and sliced into ½-inch pieces lengthwise*

1   *cup flour*

     Salt and pepper

2   *cups olive oil*

3   *cups meat sauce (see page 82)*

¾   *cup grated Parmesan cheese*

¾   *cup grated Romano cheese*

18   *(1½-ounce) slices mozzarella cheese*

Dredge the eggplant slices in the flour seasoned to taste with the salt and pepper. Heat the olive oil in a sauté pan over medium-high heat. Sauté the dredged eggplant slices until golden brown, 3 to 5 minutes per side. Set aside on paper towels to drain off the excess oil. Pat the top of the eggplant slices with another paper towel to drain the top. Preheat the oven to 400°F. In a medium casserole dish, assemble the ingredients in the following order: meat sauce, eggplant slices, Parmesan cheese, Romano cheese, and mozzarella cheese slices. Repeat the layering one more time. Bake in the oven for 20 to 25 minutes, or until the top is browned and bubbling.

MAKES 6 TO 8 SERVINGS

Marco Polo

Named Marco Polo because it goes "round the world," this dish includes some of everything including chicken, beef, veal, and sausage.

1	cup green peas	10	cloves whole garlic
4	large Idaho russet potatoes	1	teaspoon salt
1	cup olive oil	1	teaspoon pepper
1	pound mushrooms, sliced	1	tablespoon oregano
1	(4-pound) whole chicken, halved, jointed, and cut into 16 pieces	1	tablespoon granulated garlic
1½	pounds beef tenderloin, cut into 16 medallions	⅓	cup chopped parsley
		1	cup white wine
1	pound veal, cut into 16 medallions and pounded	1½	cups homemade chicken stock (page 94), or equivalent amount canned low-sodium chicken broth
2	pounds Italian rope sausage, cut into 1-inch pieces	1	cup diced Italian vinegar peppers

Preheat the oven to 375°F. Blanch the peas by placing them in boiling water for 1 minute and then rinsing them with cold water. Peel the potatoes and cut into ¼-inch wheels. In a large roasting pan, heat half of the olive oil over medium heat. Add the potatoes and sauté until they are golden brown. Turn them to ensure even cooking. Remove the potatoes from the pan. Add the mushrooms and sauté until they are soft. Remove them from the pan. Add the remaining olive oil, chicken, beef, veal, sausage, and garlic cloves to the pan and sauté lightly on all sides until all pieces of the meat are browned. Once the meats are browned, remove the garlic cloves from the pan and discard. Season the meats with the salt, pepper, oregano, garlic, and parsley. Deglaze the pan with the wine and reduce by half. Add the chicken stock and remove the roasting pan from the heat. Add the potatoes, mushrooms, and the vinegar peppers to the roasting pan. Bake in the oven for 15 to 20 minutes or until the chicken reaches an internal temperature of 155°F. To serve, arrange the potatoes around the outside of a large serving platter, place the meats in the center of the platter, and top them with the mushrooms and peppers. Pour the remaining sauce from the pan over the meats and sprinkle the peas on top. Serve immediately.

MAKES 8 TO 10 SERVINGS

Osso Buco

A specialty of Lombardy, *osso buco* literally means "bone with a hole," these vegetable-and-wine-besotted veal shanks are way more than bones. Comfort-food aficionados know *osso buco* as one of the richest and most satisfying plates of food from the Italian kitchen. Its joy comes not only from its ultrarich flavor but from the fact that it is so tender that it literally slides from the bone with the gentlest prodding of a fork.

4	pounds veal shank, washed and cut into 6 pieces
	Salt and freshly ground pepper
	Flour
⅓	cup butter
2	medium onions, diced
2	large carrots, diced
2	celery ribs, diced
6	garlic cloves, minced
1	bay leaf
2	cups white wine
2	cups homemade chicken stock (see page 94), or equivalent amount canned low-sodium chicken broth
1	pound vine-ripened tomatoes, peeled, seeded, and quartered
2	sprigs fresh thyme

Preheat the oven to 325°F. Season the veal shanks with the salt and pepper to taste and then dredge them in the flour. In a large flame-proof casserole dish or dutch oven, melt the butter over medium heat. Brown the veal shanks on each side. Remove the veal shanks from the dish and add the onions. Sauté the onions until they become translucent. Add the carrot and celery and sauté for another 5 to 6 minutes. Add the garlic and bay leaf and cook until the garlic is lightly browned, about 1 minute. Add the wine and reduce by half. Return the meat to the pan and remove from the heat. Add the chicken stock, tomatoes, and thyme. Cover and bake in the oven for 1 to 1½ hours, occasionally turning and basting the veal with the sauce. Remove the veal from the oven and remove the bay leaf and thyme from the dish.

MAKES 6 SERVINGS

Homemade Gnocchi with Roasted Red Peppers and Mushrooms

You'd think that a potato dumpling would be a fairly heavy food. Not necessarily true. Kneaded deftly, this dough yields small, featherweight dumplings we could eat all day.

FOR THE GNOCCHI:

1¼ cups all-purpose flour

2 egg yolks

½ teaspoon salt

2 pounds baked potatoes, peeled

8 cups water

1 tablespoon salt

TO ASSEMBLE THE DISH:

¼ cup olive oil

¼ cup chopped garlic

½ cup butter

¾ pound sliced mushrooms

2 red peppers, roasted and diced

2 teaspoons chopped fresh basil

½ cup homemade chicken stock (see page 94), or equivalent amount canned low-sodium chicken broth

Salt and white pepper

1½ tablespoons chopped parsley

Freshly grated Parmigiano-Reggiano or Asiago cheese

To make the gnocchi, mound the flour on a work surface and make a well in the center. Add the egg yolks and salt to the well. Put the potatoes through a potato ricer or finely grate them. Make a ring of potatoes around the flour. Knead the ingredients together quickly to form a smooth dough. Form the dough into two tubes ¾ inch in diameter. Dust the tubes with flour. Slightly flatten the tubes and then cut them into ½-inch slices. Take each piece of dough and roll it over a grater with your thumb to make a pattern on the bottom of each piece. When finished, it should resemble a dumpling. In a large stock pot, bring the water and salt to taste to a boil over high heat. Drop the gnocchi in small batches into the boiling water. When the gnocchi rise to the surface of the water, remove them with a slotted spoon and rinse. You can make the gnocchi in advance and freeze it.

To assemble the dish, heat the olive oil over medium heat in a medium saucepan. Add the garlic and sauté until the garlic is lightly browned. Add the butter and mushrooms and sauté until the mushrooms are soft. Add the roasted red peppers, gnocchi, and basil and sauté for 1 minute. Add the chicken stock and season with salt and pepper to taste. Toss with the chopped parsley. Offer freshly grated Parmigiano-Reggiano or Asiago cheese.

MAKES 4 TO 6 SERVINGS

Stuffed Sweet Red Peppers

Harry Caray's is a meat-eater's paradise, but the kitchen offers plenty of full-flavored meatless dishes, such as vegetable-stuffed red peppers.

4	large red bell peppers
1	pound stale, crusty Italian bread, crumbled
½	cup water
1	tablespoon olive oil
1	small Spanish onion, chopped
2	garlic cloves, minced
6	anchovy fillets, finely chopped
8	pitted kalamata olives, chopped
2	tablespoons extra virgin olive oil
½	teaspoon freshly ground black pepper
½	teaspoon crushed red pepper flakes
2	cups marinara sauce (see page 81) or substitute 1 (15-ounce) can tomato sauce plus ½ cup water
⅓	cup shredded Asiago cheese

Preheat the oven to 350°F. Cut off the tops of the peppers and clean and seed them. Place the peppers in a greased baking dish. Place the breadcrumbs in a large mixing bowl and sprinkle the water over them. Heat the olive oil in a medium sauté pan over low heat. Sauté the onion until translucent. Add the garlic and sauté until the garlic begins to turn brown. Combine the onion and garlic mixture with the breadcrumbs. Add the anchovies, olives, olive oil, black pepper, and red pepper flakes. Mix until well blended. Mound the stuffing into the bell peppers. Cover the bottom of the baking dish with the marinara or tomato sauce. Place the peppers upright in the baking dish, cover with foil, and bake for 45 minutes to 1 hour, or until the peppers are tender. Remove the foil, sprinkle the cheese on the peppers, and continue baking for an additional 15 minutes, basting the peppers occasionally with the sauce.

MAKES 4 SERVINGS

· SEAFOOD ·

Pan-Seared, Peppered Yellowfin Tuna
with Pinot Grigio Butter Sauce

Shrimp De Jonghe

Baked Salmon with Olives

Baked Grouper Oreganato

Plum-Glazed Salmon
with Polenta and Fried Leeks

Italian-Style Salmon

Fried Shrimp

Broiled Australian
Cold-Water Rock Lobster Tails

Pan-Seared, Peppered Yellowfin Tuna with Pinot Grigio Butter Sauce

Fruity, fresh Pinot Grigio is the basis for a refined butter sauce to dress thick tuna steaks that should be cooked only long enough to sear the exterior.

FOR THE BUTTER SAUCE:

1   cup Pinot Grigio
2   shallots, diced
2   cloves garlic, diced
½   teaspoon whole black peppercorns
¼   cup heavy cream
1½ sticks butter, cut into ½-inch slices
    Salt and pepper

FOR THE DISH:

¼   cup plus ½ tablespoon olive oil
¾   cup julienned leek stems (do not use the bulb)
6   (8-ounce) yellowfin tuna steaks
¼   cup Cajun seasoning spices
3   cups garlic mashed potatoes (see page 71)
¼   cup diced Roma tomatoes

To make the butter sauce, in a medium saucepan, combine the wine, shallots, garlic, and black peppercorns. Reduce over medium heat until syrupy. Add the heavy cream and reduce again until syrupy. With the mixture on low heat, slowly add the butter while stirring constantly. Once the butter is incorporated into the sauce, strain and add the salt and pepper to taste.

To prepare the leeks and tuna, heat ¼ cup olive oil over high heat. Fry the leeks until dark green. Drain on paper towels. Lightly coat the tuna steaks in the Cajun seasoning. Heat a dry sauté pan on high until it smokes. Roll the ½ tablespoon olive oil around the hot pan. Immediately add the tuna steaks. Sear on both sides until desired temperature is reached (medium rare is recommended, about 1 minute per side).

To serve, place ½ cup of the mashed potatoes in the center of each individual plate. Cut each tuna steak in half on a bias and arrange over the mashed potatoes. Pile the crispy leaks on top of the tuna steaks. Drizzle the Pinot Grigio butter around the mashed potatoes and sprinkle the Roma tomatoes on top of the sauce.

MAKES 6 SERVINGS

Shrimp De Jonghe

A giddy mix of breadcrumbs, sweet sherry, butter, and garlic all blanketing a cluster of shrimp, deJonghe is unique to Chicago. Historians aren't certain of its provenance, but Nancy Buckley, granddaughter of Pierre deJonghe told us that her grandfather, along with three brothers and three sisters, first served it more than a hundred years ago at the family restaurant. It is an old-fashioned-tasting dish now featured on a handful of tradition-minded Chicago menus. There's none better than Harry Caray's.

FOR THE COMPOUND BUTTER:
1   tablespoon chopped garlic
1   teaspoon Tabasco
1   tablespoon Dijon mustard
½   tablespoon lemon juice
¼   cup Japanese breadcrumbs (Panko)
1   teaspoon chopped parsley
¼   cup white wine
     Salt and white pepper
½   pound softened butter

FOR THE MARINADE:
1   tablespoon brandy
¼   cup chopped green onions
½   teaspoon Old Bay Seasoning
1   tablespoon chopped garlic
½   cup butter
1   teaspoon kosher salt
½   teaspoon black pepper
1½ pounds (size U12) headless, peeled, and
     deveined shrimp

FOR THE GARLIC BREADCRUMBS:
1   cup Japanese breadcrumbs (Panko)
⅓   cup butter
1   tablespoon chopped garlic

½   cup olive oil

To make the compound butter, combine the garlic, Tabasco, Dijon mustard, lemon juice, breadcrumbs, parsley, wine, salt and white pepper to taste, and butter. Form the mixture into a log 2 inches in diameter. Wrap in plastic and refrigerate until the butter is firm enough to slice.

In a large mixing bowl, combine the brandy, green onions, Old Bay, garlic, ¼ cup butter, salt, and black pepper. Toss the shrimp in the marinade and refrigerate for at least ½ hour.

To make the garlic breadcrumbs, pour the breadcrumbs into a medium bowl. Heat the butter in a sauté pan over medium heat and add the garlic. Sauté the garlic until brown. Strain the butter into the bowl containing the breadcrumbs.

To assemble the dish, preheat the oven to 375°F. Dredge the marinated shrimp in the garlic breadcrumbs. In a sauté pan, heat the olive oil to medium and sauté the shrimp on both sides until lightly brown. Place the sautéed shrimp in an ungreased baking dish. Cover each shrimp with thin slices of the compound butter and sprinkle with the remaining garlic breadcrumbs. Bake for 20 minutes. Serve immediately.

MAKES 4 TO 6 SERVINGS

Baked Salmon with Olives

The loud, fruity flavor of Greek kalamata olives balances the fine-textured flesh of a good salmon fillet. The combination of pastel pink fish and dark, eggplant-colored olive also has tremendous visual panache.

1	cup extra virgin olive oil
	Juice of 4 lemons
12	cloves garlic, lightly smashed
2	cups white wine
3	tablespoons finely chopped fresh Italian parsley
	Salt and pepper
4	(10-ounce) salmon fillets
8	bay leaves
1	cup kalamata olives

Preheat the oven to 350°F. In a medium bowl mix together the olive oil, lemon juice, garlic, wine, parsley, and salt and pepper to taste. Spoon half of the oil mixture into the bottom of a baking dish. Place the salmon in the dish and cover with the bay leaves and olives. Pour the remaining oil mixture over the top of the salmon. Cover the baking dish with aluminum foil and bake until the fish is opaque in the center, approximately 12 to 15 minutes. Transfer to a platter and serve.

MAKES 4 SERVINGS

SEAFOOD AT HARRY'S

Although Harry Caray's best-known and best-selling dish is steak, seafood is no second-class food group in this dining room. Such appetizers as grilled polpo (marinated baby octopus infused with spicy olive oil), shrimp Marsala, and baked clams are reminders of the restaurant's vivid Italian accent. Pillowy jumbo lump crab cakes with caper rémoulade, handsome shrimp cocktails, and freshly opened oysters on the half shell are a few other ways to start a meal with oceanic zest.

In fact, beyond the Chicago signature dish of Shrimp De Johnge, Harry's menu is replete with seafood that stars the steakhouse classic lobster tail and includes such traditional Old World dishes as linguine di mare and shrimp scampi as well as modern presentations, from plum-glazed salmon and pan-seared peppered ahi tuna to Chicago's finest crispy calamari.

Corporate Chef Garrick Dickie says that Harry's uses several sources to get its fish. "We buy from whoever has the freshest at any particular time," he explains. "Grouper comes from Florida; our Atlantic salmon is farm-

raised; the lobster tails are cold-water Australian tails, which have the firmest flesh; and our ahi tuna is 2++ grade, which is the finest other than sashimi.

"Calamari is by far the biggest seller of all our seafood," says Chef Dickie. "It's a favorite at tables and in the bar. And even people who are so-called 'fish frowners' can't stop eating it."

Baked Grouper Oreganato

Oregano is in fact a variety of marjoram, and there are some Italian-American chefs who prefer the more gentle-flavored marjoram when they make anything "oreganato," which means infused with a heavy shot of butter and herbs. Such savory cross-cultural pollination typifies Chicago's most ambitious kitchens.

---

4   (8 to 10-ounce) grouper fillets, skin removed

    Lawry's seasoned salt

    Black pepper

    Pinch of paprika

½   tablespoon oregano

½   cup lemon juice

⅓   stick thinly sliced butter

2   cups homemade chicken stock (page 94),
    or equivalent amount canned low-sodium chicken broth

1   tablespoon chopped parsley

4   parsley sprigs

4   lemon wedges

Preheat the oven to 400°F. Score the bottom of the grouper fillets in a cross-hatch pattern to keep them from curling up while baking. In a small bowl combine the salt, black pepper, paprika, and oregano. Season the fillets with the mixture and place them in a baking dish and cover with the lemon juice, butter, and chicken stock. Bake for 10 to 12 minutes. Turn the oven to broil and cook for an additional 2 minutes. Garnish with the parsley, parsley sprigs, and lemon wedges.

MAKES 4 SERVINGS

Plum-Glazed Salmon with Polenta and Fried Leeks

There are multiple stages of preparing plum-glazed salmon, but the effort yields a spectacular reward: a meal that is at once colorful and comfort food, featuring gentle textured polenta that complements almost any fresh fish.

FOR THE SALMON MARINADE:

¾ cup olive oil

1 teaspoon chopped fresh basil

1 teaspoon chopped fresh rosemary

1 teaspoon chopped fresh thyme

½ cup white wine

4 (10-ounce) salmon fillets

FOR THE PLUM GLAZE:

⅓ cup water

¼ cup sugar

1 (6-ounce) can plums

FOR THE LEMON-BUTTER SAUCE:

1 cup white wine

2 shallots, diced

Juice of ½ lemon

2 cloves garlic, diced

½ teaspoon whole black peppercorns

¼ cup heavy cream

1½ sticks butter, cut into ½-inch slices

Salt and pepper

FOR THE POLENTA:

1½ cups homemade chicken stock (see page 94), or equivalent amount canned low-sodium chicken broth

¾ cup polenta (cornmeal)

1 teaspoon chives

½ tablespoon grated Romano cheese

½ tablespoon grated Parmesan cheese

1½ cups plus 1 tablespoon olive oil

¾ cup julienned leek stems (do not use the bulb)

¼ cup diced shallots

⅓ cup diced tri-color peppers

To marinate the salmon, combine the olive oil, basil, rosemary, thyme, and wine in a medium mixing bowl. Cover the salmon with the marinade and cover and refrigerate for a minimum of 1 hour.

To make the plum glaze, in a small saucepan over medium heat combine the water, sugar, and plums. Simmer the ingredients together for 10 minutes, stirring often. Remove the mixture from the heat, allow it to cool, and then purée it in a blender or food processor.

To make the lemon-butter sauce, combine the wine, shallots, lemon juice, garlic, and peppercorns in a medium saucepan. Reduce over medium heat until syrupy. Add the heavy cream and reduce again until syrupy. With the mixture over low heat, slowly add the butter while stirring constantly. Strain. Add the salt and pepper to taste.

To make the polenta, bring the chicken stock to a boil in a medium saucepan. Stir in the polenta until the consistency is smooth and thickened. Add the chives, Romano cheese, and Parmesan cheese. Remove from the heat. Pour the polenta into a small baking dish coated with olive oil. Refrigerate for a minimum of 1 hour or until the polenta sets.

To prepare the dish, mark the marinated salmon on a grill on both sides. Preheat the oven to 350°F. Transfer the salmon to a baking dish and brush each fillet with the plum glaze. Bake for 5 to 7 minutes. Cut the polenta into ¾-inch cubes. Heat the 1½ cups olive oil over high heat and fry the polenta cubes until they are crispy. Remove the polenta cubes from the olive oil and drain on paper towels. Fry the leeks in the same sauté pan until they are dark green. Remove the leeks from the olive oil and drain them on paper towels. In another sauté pan, heat the remaining 1 tablespoon olive oil over high heat. Sauté the shallots and tri-color peppers until the shallots turn translucent.

To serve, cover the bottom of each plate with the lemon-butter sauce. Place the salmon in the center of the plate. Drizzle some of the plum glaze over the salmon. Arrange the polenta and the sautéed shallots and peppers around the salmon on each plate. Top the salmon with the fried leeks. Serve immediately.

MAKES 4 SERVINGS

Italian-Style Salmon

Italian vinegar peppers are *always* good to have on hand—to complement a cold antipasto plate, as well as to add a little pizzazz to a salmon fillet.

---

4   large Idaho russet potatoes

½   cup olive oil

4   (10-ounce) salmon fillets

1   teaspoon salt

1   teaspoon pepper

½   tablespoon oregano

1   tablespoon granulated garlic

⅓   cup chopped parsley

1½   cups white wine

1½   cups homemade chicken stock (page 94),
     or equivalent amount canned low-sodium chicken broth

8   large slices imported Italian vinegar peppers
     (reserve ½ cup vinegar)

Preheat the oven to 375°F. Peel the potatoes and cut them into quarters lengthwise. In a large roasting pan, heat the olive oil over medium heat. Add the potatoes and sauté them until golden brown, turning repeatedly, approximately 8 minutes. Add the salmon to the pan with the potatoes and sauté lightly on both sides until golden brown. Season the potatoes and the salmon with the salt, pepper, oregano, granulated garlic, and parsley. Deglaze the pan with the wine and reduce by half. Add the chicken stock and vinegar peppers (with ½ cup reserved vinegar) and put the roasting pan into the oven for 10 to 12 minutes or until the salmon reaches the desired temperature. Place the salmon on a serving plate and arrange the potatoes around the salmon. Pour the peppers and the sauce from the pan over the salmon and serve promptly.

MAKES 4 SERVINGS

Fried Shrimp

The U12-size shrimp called for in this recipe are extra large (twelve or less per pound). It is possible to substitute smaller shrimp, but only the larger shrimp can be perfectly breaded.

1½ *pounds (size U12) headless, peeled, and deveined shrimp*

1   *cup flour*

½   *teaspoon salt*

½   *teaspoon Old Bay Seasoning*

1   *cup beaten eggs*

2   *cups Japanese breadcrumbs (Panko)*

8   *cups vegetable oil*

1½ *cups cocktail sauce (see page 89)*

2   *lemons, quartered*

4   *sprigs parsley*

Butterfly the shrimp. In a small bowl, combine the flour, salt, and Old Bay. Dredge the shrimp in the seasoned flour and then in the beaten eggs and then in the breadcrumbs. In a deep sauté pan, heat the oil. Fry the shrimp in the hot oil approximately 2 minutes or until golden brown. Place a ramekin of cocktail sauce in the center of each plate. Arrange five fried shrimp around each ramekin. Garnish each plate with 2 lemon wedges and a sprig of parsley and serve immediately.

MAKES 4 SERVINGS

Broiled Australian Cold-Water Rock Lobster Tails

Here's the "surf" part of the best surf and turf—the tail of a spiny lobster. This is an entirely different creature than the Maine lobster, a.k.a. *homarus Americanus,* in that the spiny lobster has no claws. But its tail is the source of meat that is firm and rich and butter's best companion. Lobster tails are almost always sold frozen and the big ones can cost a small fortune. But there's nothing quite so luxurious as a well-prepared lobster tail that weighs in at close to a pound.

4	(12 to 14-ounce) cold water Australian rock lobster tails
	Lawry's seasoned salt
	Ground black pepper
	Pinch of paprika
	Juice of 1 lemon
1	cup clarified butter (see page 90)
1	cup homemade chicken stock (page 94), or equivalent amount canned low-sodium chicken broth
8	lemon wedges
4	sprigs parsley

Preheat the oven to 400°F. Carefully cut the top of the lobster tail shells lengthwise beginning from the base of the tail, making sure you do not cut all the way through the lobster meat. Pull the lobster meat out through the split shell from the top of the body, leaving the meat attached to the shell at the base of the tail of the lobster. Score the underside of the lobster tail meat and lay the tail meat back on top of the shell. This will keep the lobster meat from curling up during the cooking process. Season the lobster tails with the seasoned salt, black pepper, and paprika. Sprinkle the lobster tails with the lemon juice and brush them with some of the clarified butter. Place the seasoned lobster tails in a baking dish. Pour the chicken stock into the bottom of the baking dish. Bake the lobster tails in the oven for 10 to 12 minutes. Serve the lobster tails on individual plates. Garnish each plate with a ramekin of clarified butter, 2 lemon wedges, and a sprig of parsley.

MAKES 4 SERVINGS

· CHICKEN ·

Harry's Signature Chicken Vesuvio (Bone-In)

Harry's Signature Chicken Vesuvio
(Boneless Breast)

Chicken Milanese

Chicken Cacciatore

Chicken Carabina

Chicken Limone

Chicken Parmigiana

Chicken Marsala

Chicken Piccata

Chicken Italiano

Braised Chicken
with Kalamata Olives and Fresh Sage

Harry's Signature Chicken Vesuvio (Bone-In)

Voted Best Chicken Vesuvio in the City by James Ward, *ABC 7*, and Phil Vettel, *Chicago Tribune*, nowhere is this dish more essential to the culinary character of a restaurant than at Harry Caray's. The Vesuvio way of doing things is a passion in Harry's kitchen. No one seems to know exactly how Vesuvio came to be a Windy City specialty (apparently it has no real antecedents in Italy or anywhere else), and there is even conflicting speculation on how it got its name. (Our favorite explanation is that when arranged on a plate hot from the pan it looks like a huge, steaming food volcano.) Whatever its origins, it is a magical meal of chicken baked to utmost succulence encased in a red-gold crust of lush skin that slides from the meat as the meat slides off its bone. Tender? Forget about it! The dark meat in particular sets new standards for chicken tenderness.

---

1 cup frozen peas	1 tablespoon oregano
2 (4 pound) whole roasting chickens, cleaned	1 tablespoon granulated garlic
4 large Idaho russet potatoes	⅓ cup chopped parsley
½ cup olive oil	1½ cups white wine
10 whole cloves garlic	1½ cups homemade chicken stock (page 94), or equivalent amount canned low-sodium chicken broth
1 teaspoon salt	
1 teaspoon pepper	

Preheat the oven to 375°F. Blanch the peas by placing them in boiling water for 1 minute and then rinsing them with cold water to stop the cooking. Cut each chicken into eight pieces. Peel the potatoes and cut them into quarters lengthwise. In a large roasting pan, heat the olive oil over medium heat. Add the potatoes and garlic cloves and sauté the potatoes until golden brown (approximately 8 minutes). Remove the garlic cloves from the roasting pan and discard. Remove the potatoes and set aside. Add the chicken to the pan and sauté lightly on both sides until golden brown. Deglaze the pan with the wine and reduce by half. Return the potatoes to the pan. Season the potatoes and chicken with the salt, pepper, oregano, garlic, and parsley. Add the chicken stock and transfer the roasting pan to the oven for 45 minutes or until the chicken reaches an internal temperature of 155°F. Place the chicken on a serving plate and arrange the potatoes around the chicken. Pour the sauce from the pan over the chicken and sprinkle the peas on the top.

MAKES 4 SERVINGS

Harry's Signature Chicken Vesuvio (Boneless Breast)

Bone-in is the traditional Chicago way to serve chicken Vesuvio, but Harry's kitchen obliges those of us too lazy to pull meat from the bone by offering boneless breasts cooked Vesuvio style.

1	cup frozen peas	1	teaspoon pepper
4	large Idaho russet potatoes	1	tablespoon oregano
¾	cup olive oil	1	tablespoon granulated garlic
6	(7-ounce) skinless, boneless chicken breasts	⅓	cup chopped parsley
		1	cup white wine
10	whole cloves garlic	1½	cups homemade chicken stock (page 94), or equivalent amount canned low-sodium chicken broth
1	teaspoon salt		

Preheat the oven to 375°F. Blanch the peas by placing them in boiling water for 1 minute and then rinsing them with cold water to stop the cooking. Peel the potatoes and cut them into quarters lengthwise. In a large roasting pan, heat the olive oil over medium heat. Add the potatoes and sauté them until golden brown, (approximately 8 minutes). Remove the potatoes and set aside. Add the chicken and garlic to the pan and sauté lightly on both sides until golden brown. Remove the garlic cloves and discard. Deglaze the pan with the wine and reduce by half. Return the potatoes to the pan with the chicken and season with the salt, pepper, oregano, garlic, and parsley. Add the chicken stock and put the roasting pan into the oven for 15 to 20 minutes or until the chicken reaches an internal temperature of 155°F. Place the chicken on a serving plate and arrange the potatoes around the chicken. Pour the sauce from the pan over the chicken and sprinkle the peas on the top.

MAKES 6 SERVINGS

45¢ BEER

In April of 1997, when the hapless Chicago Cubs started the season with a record of 0 wins in 14 games, Harry Caray's restaurant sold fifty thousand Budweisers . . . at 45¢ apiece. The low-low price was devised to commemorate the year 1945—the year Harry Caray started his broadcasting career and the last time the Cubs won the National League pennant. The idea was to sell beer at this price until the Cubs won their first game, but no one expected their losing streak to go on as long as it did. The money-losing promotion went on so long and became such a well-known event (the lead story on ESPN five days in a row) that Las Vegas bookmakers were taking bets on how many Budweisers the restaurant would serve before the Cubs finally won.

The night after game fifteen, when the price of beer went back up to its normal $2.50 per glass, *The Tonight Show* with Jay Leno called the restaurant to congratulate it on the longest-running (and most money-losing) promotion ever!

Chicken Milanese

Milanese literally means "Milan style," referring to anything that is dipped in an egg wash and a Parmesan cheese / breadcrumb mixture, then fried in olive oil. Boneless chicken makes the most agreeable Milanese.

4	*(7-ounce) skinless, boneless chicken breasts*
2	*tablespoons milk*
2	*eggs*
¼	*cup freshly grated Parmesan cheese*
1	*tablespoon chopped parsley*
1½	*cups breadcrumbs*
	Salt and black pepper
	Flour
¾	*cup olive oil*

FOR THE LEMON BUTTER:

4	*tablespoons butter*
2	*tablespoons lemon juice*
1	*lemon, quartered*
4	*sprigs Italian parsley*

To prepare the chicken, pound the breasts to a ½-inch thickness. In a medium bowl, whisk together the milk and eggs to make an egg wash. In another bowl, combine the Parmesan cheese, parsley, breadcrumbs, and salt and black pepper to taste. Lightly flour the chicken and then dip it into the egg wash and then the seasoned breadcrumbs. In a large sauté pan, heat the olive oil over medium high heat. Add the chicken and sauté it until golden brown on both sides, about 3 minutes per side.

To make the lemon butter, in a small sauté pan melt the butter over medium heat. Add the lemon juice and stir the mixture until it is thoroughly combined.

To serve, place the chicken on four individual plates and top each chicken breast with a small amount of the lemon butter. Garnish each plate with a lemon wedge and a sprig of Italian parsley.

MAKES 4 SERVINGS

Chicken Cacciatore

Cacciatore means "hunter" in Italian, and to prepare a dish cacciatore style means to smother it with mushrooms, onions, and tomatoes, and—in Harry's recipe—olives and peppers, too.

---

6   (7-ounce) skinless, boneless chicken breasts
     Salt and black pepper
½   plus ¼ cup olive oil
1½ cups chopped Spanish onion
1½ cups sliced button mushrooms
⅔   cup sliced, pitted kalamata olives
1   cup white wine
1½ cups marinara sauce (see page 81)
1   red pepper, seeded and sliced lengthwise into 6 pieces
1   green pepper, seeded and sliced lengthwise into 6 pieces
1   yellow pepper, seeded and sliced lengthwise into 6 pieces
½   tablespoon chopped parsley

Preheat the oven to 400°F. Season the chicken breasts with the salt and pepper to taste. In a large roasting pan, heat the ½ cup olive oil over medium heat. Add the chicken breasts and sauté them on each side until golden brown. Add the onion and mushrooms and sauté until the onions are translucent. Drain away any excess olive oil still in the pan. Add the olives and deglaze the pan with the wine, simmering until the liquid is reduced by half. Add the marinara sauce and immediately remove from the stove and transfer to the oven. Bake for 15 to 20 minutes or until the chicken reaches an internal temperature of 155°F. While the chicken is baking, heat the remaining ¼ cup olive oil in a sauté pan over medium heat. Add the red, green, and yellow peppers. Season with the salt and black pepper to taste. Sauté the peppers until soft. To serve, arrange the chicken and the sauce on a large platter. Place the sautéed red, green, and yellow peppers on top of the chicken. Garnish with the chopped parsley.

MAKES 6 SERVINGS

Chicken Carabina

Harry Caray was born Harry Christopher Carabina in the Italian neighborhood of St. Louis. His childhood was not a bountiful one by any material measure. As a successful adult of means, Harry loved to go to restaurants, especially Italian restaurants. This dish was named for him and is a good expression of his zestful personality.

4 large Idaho russet potatoes	1 tablespoon oregano
½ cup olive oil	1 tablespoon granulated garlic
6 (7-ounce) skinless, boneless chicken breasts	⅓ cup chopped parsley
	1 cup white wine
1 pound sliced button mushrooms	1½ cups homemade chicken stock (page 94), or equivalent amount canned low-sodium chicken broth
10 whole cloves garlic	
1 teaspoon salt	
1 teaspoon pepper	1 cup diced imported Italian vinegar peppers

Preheat the oven to 375°F. Peel the potatoes and cut them into ¼-inch wheels. In a large roasting pan, heat the olive oil over medium heat. Add the potatoes and sauté them until golden brown (approximately 4 minutes). Remove the potatoes from the pan and set aside. Add the chicken, mushrooms, and garlic to the pan and sauté the chicken on both sides until golden brown, about 3 minutes per side. Return the potatoes to the roasting pan, arranging them around the inside edge of the pan (around the chicken). Season the potatoes, mushrooms, and chicken with the salt, pepper, oregano, garlic, and parsley. Deglaze the pan with the wine and reduce by half. Remove the garlic cloves and add the chicken stock and the vinegar peppers. Put the roasting pan in the oven for 15 to 20 minutes or until the chicken reaches an internal temperature of 155°F. Place the chicken on a serving plate and arrange the potatoes around the chicken. Pour the sauce from the pan over the chicken and serve.

MAKES 6 SERVINGS

Chicken Limone

Pollo al limone is a traditional Tuscan dish, often made with white wine and olive oil. Harry Caray's recipe eliminates the wine and adds plenty of butter, but there is no changing the essential lemon flavoring. Use fresh lemon juice, preferably from the most plump, ripe lemons you can find.

½   cup plus 2 tablespoons butter

2   tablespoons flour

4½ cups homemade chicken stock (page 94),
    or equivalent amount canned low-sodium chicken broth

4   (7-ounce) skinless, boneless chicken breasts
    Salt and white pepper
    Flour

4   eggs

6   tablespoons lemon juice

1   lemon, sliced into wheels

1   tablespoon chopped parsley

In a small sauté pan over medium heat melt the 2 tablespoons butter. Add the flour and stir until the roux is a peanut butter consistency, 1 to 2 minutes. Remove from the heat. In a medium saucepan over high heat, bring the chicken stock to a boil. Whisk in the roux and continue to whisk over the heat until the stock thickens, 2 to 3 minutes. Season the chicken breasts with salt and white pepper to taste. Dredge them in the flour. Beat the eggs in a medium mixing bowl. In a sauté pan, melt ½ cup butter over medium heat. Dip the floured chicken breasts into the eggs. Sauté the chicken breasts on both sides until lightly brown, about 3 minutes per side. Remove the chicken from the sauté pan and place it in a baking dish. Preheat the oven to 375°F. Deglaze the sauté pan with the lemon juice. Add the thickened chicken stock and salt and white pepper to taste. Pour the mixture over the chicken breasts and bake in the oven for 15 minutes. Garnish with the lemon wheels and parsley.

MAKES 4 SERVINGS

Chicken Parmigiana

Chicken Parmigiana is not a classic Italian dish, but it has long been one of the most popular Italian-American preparations, found everywhere from inside a hero sandwich to atop a fine china plate in a linen-tablecloth restaurant.

1½ cups breadcrumbs
1   teaspoon oregano
1   teaspoon basil
1   teaspoon salt
½   teaspoon pepper
1   teaspoon granulated garlic
6   (7-ounce) skinless, boneless chicken breasts
1   cup flour
1   cup beaten eggs
1   cup olive oil
3   cups meat sauce (see page 82)
⅓   cup grated Parmesan cheese
⅓   cup grated Romano cheese
12 (2-ounce) slices mozzarella cheese

Preheat the oven to 400°F. Combine the breadcrumbs, oregano, basil, salt, pepper, and garlic. Dredge the chicken breasts in the flour, then the beaten eggs, and then the seasoned breadcrumbs. Heat the olive oil over medium-high heat in a large sauté pan. Sauté the breaded chicken breasts on each side until golden brown, about 3 minutes per side. Place the chicken in a baking dish and top with the meat sauce. Sprinkle the Parmesan and Romano cheeses on each breast. Bake for 12 to 15 minutes to an internal temperature of at least 155°F. Remove from the oven and turn the oven to broil. Place 2 slices of the mozzarella on each chicken breast and broil until the cheese is melted, about 3 minutes. Arrange the chicken breasts on a platter and serve.

MAKES 6 SERVINGS

Chicken Marsala

Gravy made from pan drippings and Marsala wine make almost any entrée taste special. When you add the wine to deglaze the pan, be sure to scrape up all the bits of chicken.

¾ cup plus 1 tablespoon butter

1 cup plus 1 tablespoon flour

2 cups homemade chicken stock (page 94),
   or equivalent amount canned low-sodium chicken broth

6 (7-ounce) skinless, boneless chicken breasts

½ teaspoon salt

½ teaspoon black pepper

1½ pounds button mushrooms, sliced

1 cup Marsala wine

Place an ovenproof plate in the oven and preheat it to 200°F. In a small sauté pan melt 1 tablespoon of butter over medium heat. Add 1 tablespoon flour and stir the roux until it is a peanut butter consistency, 1 to 2 minutes, and then remove from the heat. In a medium saucepan over high heat, bring the chicken stock to a boil. Whisk in the roux and continue to whisk over the heat until the stock thickens, 2 to 3 minutes, and set aside. Season the chicken breasts with the salt and pepper. Dredge the chicken in the remaining flour. Melt the ¾ cup butter in a large sauté pan over medium heat. Brown the chicken on both sides, 2½ to 3 minutes per side. Remove the chicken to the plate in the oven. Add the mushrooms and sauté until the mushrooms are soft. Remove the mushrooms and set aside, reserving all the liquid in the pan. Deglaze the pan with the wine. Add the chicken stock and return the mushrooms to the pan. Sauté for 2 minutes to heat the mushrooms. Pour the sauce over the chicken and serve.

MAKES 6 SERVINGS

Chicken Piccata

This sauce is made from a flour, lemon, and butter sauce with just a bit of extra sparkle in the form of capers.

½   cup plus 2 tablespoons butter

1   cup plus 2 tablespoons flour

4   (7-ounce) skinless, boneless chicken breasts

     Salt and white pepper

4   eggs

4½ cups homemade chicken stock (see page 94),
     or equivalent amount canned low-sodium chicken broth

6   tablespoons lemon juice

2   tablespoons capers

1   lemon, sliced into wheels

1   tablespoon chopped parsley

Preheat the oven to 375°F. In a small sauté pan melt 2 tablespoons of butter over medium heat. Add 2 tablespoons of flour and stir until the roux has a peanut butter consistency, 1 to 2 minutes, and remove from the heat. In a medium saucepan over high heat, bring the chicken stock to a boil. Whisk in the roux and continue to whisk over the heat until the stock thickens, 2 to 3 minutes, and set aside. Season the chicken breasts with salt and white pepper to taste. Dredge them in the remaining flour. In a medium mixing bowl, beat the eggs. In a sauté pan, melt the ½ cup butter over medium heat. Dip the floured chicken breasts into the eggs. Sauté the chicken breasts on both sides until lightly brown, about 3 minutes per side. Remove the chicken from the sauté pan and place in a baking dish. Deglaze the sauté pan with the lemon juice. Add the thickened chicken stock, the capers and salt and white pepper to taste. Pour the sauce over the chicken breasts and bake in the oven for 15 minutes. Garnish with the lemon wheels and parsley.

MAKES 4 SERVINGS

Chicken Italiano

This is called chicken Italiano not only because of its flavors, but because each boneless breast wraps a filling of green, red, and white like the Italian flag. Chip Caray and Skip Caray cooked this chicken Italiano dish for a Food Network special, *Best of Sports Star Eats,* shot in Harry Caray's kitchen.

4	(7-ounce) skinless, boneless chicken breasts
	Salt and pepper
1	cup sautéed spinach
1	roasted red pepper, peeled and quartered
½	pound goat cheese
¾	cup grated Parmesan cheese
	Flour
4	eggs
¼	cup milk
2	cups breadcrumbs
4	teaspoons chopped Italian parsley
⅓	cup grated Romano cheese
2	teaspoons granulated garlic
¾	cup olive oil

Preheat the oven to 350°F. Pound the chicken breasts to ¼-inch thickness and season them with salt and pepper to taste. Top each chicken breast with one-fourth of the spinach, the red pepper, goat cheese, and Parmesan cheese. Roll the chicken breasts with the ingredients inside. Secure each breast with a toothpick. Lightly dust the rolled chicken breasts with flour. In a small bowl, whisk the eggs and milk together. In a medium bowl, combine the breadcrumbs, parsley, Romano cheese, garlic, and salt and pepper to taste. Dip the floured chicken in the egg wash and then roll it in the seasoned breadcrumbs. Heat a sauté pan to medium and add the olive oil. Lightly sauté the chicken on both sides until golden brown. Place the chicken in a casserole dish and bake in the oven for 12 to 15 minutes or until the chicken reaches an internal temperature of 155°F.

MAKES 4 SERVINGS

Braised Chicken with Kalamata Olives and Fresh Sage

Braising means to brown meat, then cover it and simmer slowly in a small amount of liquid. It results in utmost tenderness and a powerful flavor bouquet.

---

2   *(4-pound) whole roasting chickens, cleaned*
   Salt and pepper
   Flour
¼   *cup olive oil*
¼   *cup butter*
6   *garlic cloves, finely chopped*
12 *small sage leaves*
2   *cups white wine*
2   *cups homemade chicken stock (see page 94),*
   or equivalent amount canned low-sodium chicken broth
1½ *cups pitted and sliced kalamata olives*

Cut each chicken into eight pieces. Season the chicken with salt and pepper to taste. Dredge the chicken in the flour. Heat the olive oil and butter in a large sauté pan over medium-high heat. Brown each piece of chicken on both sides. Add the garlic and sage leaves and fry them with the chicken until the garlic begins to brown. Deglaze the pan with the wine, reduce by half, and add the chicken stock. Cover the pan, reduce the heat, and simmer for 20 minutes. Add the olives and simmer for another 20 minutes. Season the chicken with salt and pepper to taste. Serve.

MAKES 6 TO 8 SERVINGS

• STEAKS, VEAL • & CHOPS

Harry's Signature New York Strip,
Peppercorn Style

Italian Steak Pizziola

Beef Filet Wrapped in Pancetta

Bone-In Rib-Eye Steak

Veal Parmigiana

Veal Piccata

Veal Scaloppine

Veal Marsala

Veal Chops with Peppers and Onions

Lamb Chops Oreganato

Lamb Chops with Mint Jelly

Grilled Pork Chops with Applesauce

Pork Chops, Italian Syle

Stuffed Italian Pork Chops

Surf and Turf

Beef Tenderloin Tips
with Gorgonzola Cheese and Roma Tomatoes

Harry's Signature
New York Strip, Peppercorn Style

There is no city more serious about steak than Chicago, and no restaurant in Chicago more devoted to steak than Harry Caray's. This was Harry's favorite way to eat the prime sirloin strip.

---

4   (16-ounce) prime New York strip steaks
1   cup dry English mustard
1   cup cracked black peppercorns
2   cups bordelaise sauce (see page 93)
    Parsley sprigs

Preheat the oven to 400°F. Lightly coat both sides of the steaks with the mustard. Lay the cracked black peppercorns out on the countertop or plate and press the steaks into the peppercorns so they coat the meat. Place the steaks on a hot grill for 1 minute on each side (or on an ungreased cookie sheet and broil for 1 minute on each side). Cook the steaks in the oven until desired temperature is reached. Remove the steaks from the oven and allow them to rest for 2 to 3 minutes so they retain their juiciness. In a saucepan over medium heat, warm the bordelaise sauce. Slice the steaks on a bias into ¾-inch pieces, but don't slice all of the way through. Pour the warm bordelaise sauce over the top of the steaks. Garnish with the parsley sprigs and serve immediately.

MAKES 4 SERVINGS

BEEF

When you come to Harry Caray's for steak, you not only eat a great one; you get a beef education. As has long been a Chicago custom, the meal begins with the server showing you a tray crowded with cuts of steak, chops, and lobster in the raw (wrapped in cellophane). You can study the grain of the meat and its marbling. The marbling in the meat are the thin veins of fat running throughout. It's what gives the meat its flavor, tenderness, and juiciness and is sometimes injected into the steak. He'll explain to you that the filet mignon is, of course, the most tender; the T-bone combines that tender tenderloin with a somewhat firmer piece of top loin; the porterhouse is basically a T-bone but with more of the tenderloin on the bone; and a New York strip is not quite as tender, but is juicier and more beefy in flavor.

What you *cannot* see on the waiter's tray is the way the beef is cared for even before it reaches the kitchen. Using only cuts from the approximately 2 percent that is graded prime, Harry Caray's serves steaks that virtually burst with juice and flavor when their darkened crust is severed with a knife. Matt Pollack of Stock Yards (www.stockyards.com), the one hundred-plus-year-old company that supplies all of the restaurant's beef, explained why these steaks are so especially delicious. "We know our sources; we know the breeding and the feeding; we like the corn and grain that Midwest cattle get."

Pollack scoffed at cattle from hotter regions, explaining that "when it's warm, animals drink more and eat less, meaning they don't grade out as high." *Grade out* refers to the ranking of beef by the USDA according to its general appearance, but most importantly how it is marbled, i.e. how richly the fat is distributed in the lean. Prime is the best grade, given to only about 2 percent of beef; and it is the only grade that Harry Caray's uses. Pollack said that much of the prime beef supplied to the restaurant is from the heartland's Angus cows, which marble earlier and finer. Steaks from these cows are wet aged a minimum of three weeks, turning especially tender. Such meat is simply impossible to find in a grocery store because "at the supermarket, you get a fresh-cut steak," explained Pollack. "Most grocers need to move what they have and move it fast. Aging makes all the difference. We are sitting on six million dollars' worth of meat at any one time." So when Harry Caray's gets its steak, it has developed tenderness and flavor that only time—and *prime*—can produce.

There are many good and true-Chicago things to eat on Harry Caray's menu, including the city's definitive chicken Vesuvio and pastas on a par with the city's best; but more than one out of five dinner customers come to eat steak. The best-selling entrée by far is the nine-ounce filet mignon, which accounts for about 15 percent of all dinners. The second best-seller is the thirteen-ounce filet. Number three is the New York sirloin crusted with peppercorns.

Beef Cooking Temperatures	
Rare	120°F
Medium Rare	130°F
Medium	140°F
Medium Well	150°F
Well Done	170°F+

Italian Steak Pizziola

To dress up beef, Italian-style, Harry's offers a heady relish concocted from peppers and onions.

4	*(16-ounce) prime New York strip steaks*
	Lawry's seasoned salt
	Black pepper
¼	*cup olive oil*
1	*green pepper, cleaned, seeded, and julienned*
1	*red pepper, cleaned, seeded, and julienned*
1	*yellow pepper, cleaned, seeded, and julienned*
6	*cloves garlic, chopped*
1	*medium onion, peeled and sliced*
	Pinch of crushed red pepper
½	*cup red wine*
2	*cups diced tomatoes*
1	*teaspoon oregano*
1	*tablespoon chopped parsley*

Preheat the oven to 400°F. Season the steaks with the Lawry's seasoned salt and black pepper. Mark the steaks on a grill (or broil in the oven on each side for 1 minute). Transfer the steaks to a baking dish and bake until they reach the desired temperature. In a large sauté pan, heat the olive oil over medium heat. Add the julienned peppers, garlic, onion, and red pepper. Sauté together for 2 minutes or until the onions become translucent. Deglaze the pan by adding the red wine. Add the tomatoes, oregano, and parsley. Reduce the heat and simmer for 5 minutes until the sauce reduces slightly. To serve, simply top the steaks with the tomato, pepper, and onion mixture.

MAKES 4 BIG SERVINGS

Beef Filet Wrapped in Pancetta

Because the tenderloin of beef is less fully marbled than other cuts, it benefits from the infusion of pancetta-wrap juices that melt into it as it cooks.

---

1   *(2-pound) fully trimmed whole beef tenderloin*
1   *tablespoon kosher salt*
3   *tablespoons whole grain Dijon mustard*
⅓   *pound pancetta, thinly sliced*

Preheat the oven to 400°F. Rub the tenderloin with the kosher salt. Coat the tenderloin evenly with the Dijon mustard. Wrap the pancetta slices around the tenderloin, covering it completely. Tie the pancetta in place with twine. Place the tenderloin on a rack in a roasting pan and put it in the oven. Roast for 20 minutes. Turn the oven off and leave the tenderloin in the oven for another 15 minutes. Snip and remove the twine and slice the tenderloin into thick slices. Arrange the slices on a large platter and serve immediately.

MAKES 4 SERVINGS

Bone-In Rib-Eye Steak

Harry Caray's has a very specific way of cooking steaks. They are first put on the grill to sear the outside and thereby seal in the juices. After being "marked" in this fashion, the steaks are baked in a convection oven to attain the exact degree of desired doneness. The result: maximum juiciness and flavor.

---

4   (23-ounce) prime, 1-inch, Frenched,
    bone-in, rib-eye steaks, cut thick

    Lawry's seasoned salt

    Black pepper

Prepare a grill, or turn the oven to broil. Season the steaks with the salt and black pepper to taste. Mark the steaks on a grill, or broil in the oven, on each side for 1 minute. Preheat the oven to 400°F, or if broiling turn the oven to bake at 400°F. Transfer the steaks to a baking dish and bake until they reach the desired temperature. Serve immediately.

MAKES 4 SERVINGS

Veal Parmigiana

To make really wonderful veal parmigiana you need to get the best quality tender veal. Sauté it only long enough for it to turn golden brown and sprinkle it with freshly grated Parmesan and Romano cheeses, then use creamy mozzarella on top. The result is a classic Italian-American dish that tastes somehow familiar, but wows the palate.

1½ cups breadcrumbs
1   teaspoon oregano
1   teaspoon basil
1   teaspoon salt
½   teaspoon pepper
1   teaspoon granulated garlic
2   pounds veal, trimmed of all fat
1   cup flour
1   cup beaten eggs
1   cup olive oil
3   cups meat sauce (see page 82)
⅓   cup grated Parmesan cheese
⅓   cup grated Romano cheese
12 (2-ounce) slices mozzarella cheese

Preheat the oven to broil. Combine the breadcrumbs, oregano, basil, salt, pepper, and garlic. Cut the veal into six pieces and pound them to ¼-inch thickness. Heat the olive oil in a large sauté pan over medium heat. Dredge the veal in the flour, then the egg, then the seasoned breadcrumbs. Sauté the breaded veal on each side until golden brown, about 2 minutes per side. Heat the meat sauce in a medium pot over medium heat. Place the veal in a baking dish and cover with the meat sauce. Sprinkle the Parmesan and Romano cheeses on each piece of veal. Place 2 slices of the mozzarella on each piece of veal and broil until the cheese is melted, 2 to 3 minutes. Arrange the veal on a large serving platter and serve.

MAKES 4 TO 6 SERVINGS

Veal Piccata

Quickly sautéed and served with a sauce made from pan drippings, lemon juice, and chopped parsley, veal piccata is an Italian restaurant classic. You can also prepare breasts of chicken in the same manner (see page 158).

½   *cup plus 1½ tablespoons butter*

1   *cup plus 1½ tablespoons flour*

3   *cups homemade chicken stock (page 94),*
    or equivalent amount canned low-sodium chicken broth

2   *pounds veal, trimmed of all fat*
    Salt and white pepper

4½   *tablespoons lemon juice*

2   *tablespoons capers*

1   *lemon, sliced into wheels*

1   *tablespoon chopped parsley*

In a small sauté pan melt the 1½ tablespoons butter over medium heat. Add the 1½ tablespoons flour and stir until the roux has a peanut butter consistency, 1 to 2 minutes, and remove from the heat. In a medium saucepan over high heat, bring the chicken stock to a boil. Whisk in the roux and continue to whisk over the heat until the stock thickens, 2 to 3 minutes, and set aside. Cut the veal into 16 pieces and pound them to ¼-inch thickness. Season the veal with the salt and white pepper to taste. Dredge the veal in the 1 cup flour. In a sauté pan, melt ½ cup butter over medium heat. Sauté the veal on both sides until lightly brown, about 1 minute per side. Remove the veal from the sauté pan and place on a serving platter. Deglaze the pan with the lemon juice. Add the chicken stock, capers, and salt and white pepper to taste. Return the veal to the pan and simmer the mixture for 2 minutes and garnish with the lemon wheels and chopped parsley.

MAKES 4 TO 6 SERVINGS

Veal Scaloppine

Scaloppine means a thin scallop of meat—in this case, veal—and it is usually prepared by dredging it in flour before sautéing. Scaloppine dishes are traditionally served with a sauce based on tomatoes, and Harry Caray's version adds diced vegetables for extra color.

1½ pounds veal, trimmed of all fat
    Salt and white pepper
    Flour
½   cup butter
1   yellow onion, finely diced
1   zucchini, finely diced
1   yellow squash, finely diced
1   medium red pepper, seeded and finely diced
1   medium green pepper, seeded and finely diced
1   medium yellow pepper, seeded and finely diced
½   cup white wine
1   cup marinara sauce (see page 81)
1   cup homemade chicken stock (page 94),
    or equivalent amount canned low-sodium chicken broth
1   tablespoon chopped Italian parsley

Cut the veal into 16 pieces and pound them to ¼-inch thickness. Season the veal with the salt and pepper to taste. Dredge the veal in the flour. Heat the butter in a large sauté pan over medium heat. Brown the veal on both sides, about 1 minute per side, and remove the veal from the pan. Add the onion, zucchini, yellow squash, and the tri-color peppers. Sauté until the vegetables begin to soften. Deglaze the pan with the wine and reduce by half. Add the marinara sauce and chicken stock and simmer for 6 to 8 minutes. Return the veal to the sauté pan and simmer for 2 more minutes. Salt and pepper to taste. Arrange the veal and sauce on a large platter or on individual plates and sprinkle with the chopped parsley.

MAKES 4 TO 6 SERVINGS

THANKSGIVING FOR ORPHANS

Harry Caray had a sad childhood. Born Harry Christopher Carabina in St. Louis in 1914, he never knew his father, who abandoned him at birth. He grew up poor, selling newspapers for a few cents a day; and when he was eight years old, his mother died. His stepfather, who ran a restaurant, couldn't keep him. So Harry was raised by his aunt Doxie, whose husband also left her alone, a single mother with four kids plus Harry. It was a lonely time; and later, when revisiting St. Louis with Steve Stone, he commented, "When you don't know your mother or your father or any of your relatives, it's a tough row to hoe."

Because of the sadness of his youth, Harry had a special place in his heart for orphans; and out of that concern, Harry Caray's restaurant has always been a supporter of the Maryville Youth Academy in suburban Chicago. In addition to financial contributions over the years, Harry Caray's annually hosts a Thanksgiving dinner for five hundred children from Maryville, aged eight to seventeen. It's a feast of turkey with all the trimmings and appearances by Santa and Mrs. Claus (complete with Christmas presents for everyone), the Holy Cow, a performance by the Blues Brothers, and

(Clockwise from left): Santa Clause, Richard Dent (Bears Superbowl XX MVP), Marv Levy (Hall of Fame Former Buffalo Bills Coach), Grant DePorter (Harry Caray's managing partner), Father John P. Smyth (executive director of Maryville), Dutchie Caray, and two children from Maryville

visits from sports-star friends of Harry's. Before his death, Harry always either appeared at the event or called in to lead everyone in singing "Take Me Out to the Ball Game."

When Harry died in February 1998, the entire staff of the restaurant pooled their tips and handed the sum to Maryville; and later that year, in July, the restaurant donated one thousand dollars to the orphanage for every home run Sammy Sosa hit.

Veal Marsala

Marsala is Italy's best-known fortified wine, frequently served for dessert. Here its smoky-rich flavor adds punch to fragile-flavored veal.

¾   cup plus 1 tablespoon butter

1   cup plus 1 tablespoon flour

2   cups homemade chicken stock (page 94),
     or equivalent amount canned low-sodium chicken broth

2   pounds veal, trimmed of all fat

½   teaspoon salt

½   teaspoon black pepper

1½   pounds button mushrooms, sliced

1   cup Marsala wine

In a small sauté pan melt 1 tablespoon butter over medium heat. Add 1 tablespoon flour and stir until the roux has a peanut butter consistency, 1 to 2 minutes, and remove from the heat. In a medium saucepan over high heat, bring the chicken stock to a boil. Whisk in the roux and continue to whisk over the heat until the stock thickens, 2 to 3 minutes, and set aside. Cut the veal into 16 pieces and pound them to ¼-inch thickness. Season the veal with the salt and pepper. Dredge the veal in the remaining flour. Melt the ¾ cup butter in a large sauté pan over medium heat. Brown the veal on both sides and remove the veal from the pan. Add the mushrooms to the sauté pan and sauté until they are soft. Remove the mushrooms from the pan and set aside, reserving the liquid in the pan. Deglaze the pan with the wine. Add the chicken stock, return the mushrooms and the veal to the pan, and simmer until the veal is warmed through.

MAKES 4 TO 6 SERVINGS

Veal Chops with Peppers and Onions

The big veal chop is king of meat in Italian restaurants. Harry Caray's serves massive one-pounders that are so tender that a knife seems to fall through them.

---

4   (16-ounce) veal chops
    Lawry's seasoned salt
    Black pepper
½   cup olive oil
2   yellow onions, sliced into ½-inch wheels
1   red bell pepper, seeded and sliced into 8 pieces
1   yellow bell pepper, seeded and sliced into 8 pieces
1   green bell pepper, seeded and sliced into 8 pieces
½   cup white wine
1   cup homemade chicken stock (page 94),
    or equivalent amount canned low-sodium chicken broth
1   tablespoon chopped parsley
    Salt and black pepper

Season the veal chops with salt and black pepper to taste. Mark the veal chops on a grill or broil in the oven on each side for 2 minutes. Preheat the oven to 400°F. In a large sauté pan, heat the olive oil over medium heat. Add the onions, red peppers, yellow peppers, and green peppers and sauté until the onions become translucent. Deglaze the pan with the white wine. Add the chicken stock, parsley, and salt and pepper to taste. Transfer the veal chops to a casserole dish and cover with the pepper and onion mixture. Bake until the veal chops reach the desired degree of doneness.

MAKES 4 SERVINGS

Lamb Chops Oreganato

Like beef, lamb is USDA-graded into prime, choice, good, and utility. Harry Caray's uses prime Colorado domestic lamb rather than New Zealand or Australian lamb. The domestic lamb has a larger eye and more meat. It's also less gamy than ones from overseas. That's one good reason its lamb chops are the best in Chicago.

12   *(6-ounce) Colorado lamb chops, trimmed and Frenched*

      Lawry's seasoned salt

      Black pepper

2   *tablespoons oregano*

⅓   *cup lemon juice*

2   *cups homemade chicken stock (page 94),
or equivalent amount canned low-sodium chicken broth*

1   *tablespoon chopped parsley*

      Parsley sprigs

Preheat the oven to broil. Season the lamb chops with the salt and black pepper to taste. Place the lamb chops eye side up in a baking pan. Sprinkle the top of the lamb chops with the oregano and place under the broiler for 15 to 20 seconds until the oregano is toasted. Turn the lamb chops over and repeat the process. Change the oven setting to bake at 400°F. Pour the lemon juice over the lamb chops. Cover the bottom of the pan with the chicken stock. Sprinkle with the chopped parsley. Bake until the desired temperature is reached. When finished, arrange the lamb chops on a large platter. Cover them with the pan juices and garnish with parsley sprigs.

MAKES 4 TO 6 SERVINGS

Lamb Chops with Mint Jelly

A Frenched lamb chop is one on which the meat at the tip is cut away to expose the bone. This leaves a small circle of meat that is tender, gentle-flavored, and supremely juicy. It used to be customary to dress the bone of each Frenched chop with little frilly paper panties so it could be picked up without getting juice on your fingers. Nowadays, most people don't mind a little finger-licking as part of the lamb-chop-eating ritual.

12 (6-ounce) Colorado lamb chops, trimmed and Frenched
  Lawry's seasoned salt
  Ground black pepper
1 cup mint jelly

Prepare a grill, or turn the oven to broil. Season the lamb chops with the salt and black pepper to taste. Mark the lamb chops on a grill, or broil in the oven, on each side for 2 minutes. Preheat the oven to 400°F. Transfer the lamb chops to a baking dish and bake until they reach the desired temperature. Serve with a side of mint jelly.

MAKES 4 SERVINGS

Grilled Pork Chops with Applesauce

Perhaps the most important thing when cooking pork chops (other than getting good quality chops to begin with) is not to overcook them. They need to be cooked through, but not so much that they lose their characteristic succulence.

---

12   *(6-ounce) 1-inch-thick, semiboneless pork chops*
     Lawry's seasoned salt
     Ground black pepper
1   *cup applesauce*

Prepare a grill, or turn the oven to broil. Season the pork chops with the salt and black pepper to taste. Mark the pork chops on a grill or broil in the oven on each side for 2 minutes. Preheat the oven to 400°F. Transfer the pork chops to a baking dish and bake until they reach the desired temperature. Serve with a side of applesauce.

MAKES 6 TO 8 SERVINGS

Pork Chops, Italian Style

Don't feel limited to pork chops. "Italian Style" is also a great preparation for any steak, chop or chicken. In this recipe the savor of vinegar peppers adds a sharp tang to the mild sweetness of the pork.

4	large Idaho russet potatoes
½	cup olive oil
12	(6-ounce) 1-inch-thick semiboneless pork chops
10	cloves garlic
1	teaspoon salt
1	teaspoon pepper
2	teaspoons oregano
1	tablespoon granulated garlic
⅓	cup chopped parsley
1	cup white wine
1½	cups homemade chicken stock (page 94), or equivalent amount canned low-sodium chicken broth
8	large slices imported Italian peppers in vinegar (reserve ½ cup vinegar)

Preheat the oven to 375°F. Peel the potatoes and cut into quarters lengthwise. In a large roasting pan, heat the olive oil over medium heat. Add the potatoes and sauté them until golden brown, turning repeatedly, approximately 8 minutes. Remove the potatoes and set aside. Add the pork chops and garlic to the pan and sauté on both sides until golden brown, 2 to 3 minutes per side. Return the potatoes to the pan and season them and the pork chops with the salt, pepper, oregano, granulated garlic, and parsley. Deglaze the pan with the white wine. Remove the garlic cloves and discard. Add the chicken stock, the vinegar peppers (with ½ cup reserved vinegar) and put the roasting pan into the oven for 15 to 20 minutes or until the pork chops reach the desired degree of doneness. Place the pork chops on a serving plate and arrange the potatoes around the pork chops. Spoon the peppers and the sauce from the pan over the pork chops.

MAKES 6 TO 8 SERVINGS

Stuffed Italian Pork Chops

Although a plain grilled pork chop done right is wonderful, sometimes it's fun to gild the lily.

---

8   (6-ounce) 1-inch-thick boneless pork chops

    Salt

    White pepper

8   *thin slices mozzarella*

8   *thin slices prosciutto, diced*

2   *eggs, beaten*

1   *cup breadcrumbs*

¼   *cup olive oil*

4   *sprigs Italian parsley*

Preheat the oven to 400°F. Season the pork chops with salt and pepper to taste. Slice a pocket in each pork chop. Stuff each chop with a slice of mozzarella and a slice of prosciutto. Dip the chops into the beaten eggs and then roll them in the breadcrumbs. Heat the olive oil in a large sauté pan over medium heat and sauté the chops until they are golden brown on all sides, about 3 minutes per side. Place the chops on a cookie sheet and bake in the oven for 15 to 20 minutes or until the chops are the desired temperature. Serve two chops per plate and garnish with a parsley sprig.

MAKES 4 TO 6 SERVINGS

Surf and Turf

The big lobster tails called for in this recipe tend to be very pricey, more so even than prime filet mignon; but that's the point of surf and turf. It is essential to any topflight steakhouse menu because it is the height of luxury—two of nature's richest foods combined on a single plate.

---

4 *(9-ounce) beef tenderloins (filet mignons)*

Lawry's seasoned salt

Ground black pepper

4 *(12- to 14-ounce) cold-water Australian rock lobster tails*

Paprika

Juice of 1 lemon

1 *cup clarified butter (see page 90)*

1 *cup homemade chicken stock (page 94), or equivalent amount canned low-sodium chicken broth*

8 *lemon wedges*

4 *sprigs parsley*

Prepare a grill, or turn the oven to broil. Season the tenderloins with the seasoned salt and black pepper to taste. Mark the tenderloins on a grill, or broil in the oven, on each side for 1 minute. Place the tenderloins in a baking dish and set aside.

Preheat the oven to 400°F. Carefully cut the top of the lobster tail shells lengthwise beginning from the base of the tail, making sure you do not cut all the way through the lobster meat. Pull the lobster meat out through the split shell from the top of the body, leaving the meat attached to the shell at the tail of the lobster. Score the underside of the lobster tail meat and lay the tail meat back on top of the shell. This will keep the lobster meat from curling up during the cooking process. Season the lobster tails with the seasoned salt, black pepper, and a pinch of paprika. Sprinkle the lobster tails with lemon juice and brush them with some of the clarified butter. Place the seasoned lobster tails in a separate baking dish. Pour the chicken stock into the bottom of the baking dish. Bake the lobster tails in the oven for 10 to 12 minutes. Bake the tenderloins in the oven to the desired temperature. Serve on individual platters with one filet and one lobster tail on each plate. Garnish each platter with a ramekin of clarified butter, 2 lemon wedges, and a sprig of parsley.

MAKES 4 SERVINGS

Beef Tenderloin Tips with Gorgonzola Cheese and Roma Tomatoes

Beef, cheese, and a rich bordelaise sauce: not a meal you necessarily want to eat every day. But on those occasions when maximum satisfaction is required, this dish fills the bill.

2   *pounds beef tenderloin tips*
    Lawry's seasoned salt
    Ground black pepper
½   *cup olive oil*
2   *cups bordelaise sauce (see page 93)*
1   *cup diced Roma tomatoes*
1   *cup crumbled Gorgonzola cheese*

Season the beef tenderloin with the seasoned salt and black pepper. In a large sauté pan, heat the olive oil over a medium-high heat. Sear the tenderloin tips in the olive oil until they are brown on all sides, 1 to 2 minutes. Add the bordelaise sauce, reduce the heat, and simmer for 10 minutes. Toss the Roma tomatoes in the sauté pan and remove the pan from the heat. Place the tips and sauce on a serving dish and sprinkle with the Gorgonzola cheese. Serve immediately.

MAKES 4 TO 6 SERVINGS

• DESSERTS •

Key Lime Pie

Hot Fudge Brownie Sundaes

Fresh Berries with Zabaglione

Cannoli

Carrot Cake with Cream Cheese Frosting

Lemon Cheesecake

Chocolate Chip Cheesecake

Chocolate Tortas
with Warm Caramel Pecan Sauce

Crème Brûlée

Crème Anglaise

Mini Warm Apple Pies
with Apple Cinnamon Ice Cream

Key Lime Pie

To serve Key lime pie Harry Caray style, cut it into very large portions! A good source for real Key lime juice is the Key West Key Lime Shop (www.keylimeshop.com).

FOR THE CRUST:

1   cup graham cracker crumbs

½   cup finely chopped walnuts

    Dash of ground cinnamon

1½ tablespoons brown sugar

7   to 8 tablespoons melted butter

FOR THE FILLING:

2   egg yolks

1   whole egg

    Dash of salt

3   tablespoons sugar

½   cup key lime juice

    Dash of vanilla

1¾ cups sweetened condensed milk

3   egg whites

    Whipped cream

6   mint leaves

1   lime, cut into 6 wheels

To make the crust, preheat the oven to 325°F. Combine the graham cracker crumbs, walnuts, cinnamon, and brown sugar in a large mixing bowl. Slowly add the melted butter 1 tablespoon at a time until the mixture binds together. Press the mixture into a 9-inch pie pan and refrigerate until ready to use.

To make the filling, in a medium bowl whisk the egg yolks, whole egg, salt, sugar, key lime juice, vanilla, and sweetened condensed milk. In a separate bowl, whip the egg whites with a hand mixer until they thicken and form soft peaks. Slowly fold the egg whites into the condensed milk mixture. Pour the combined mixture into the pie shell and bake in the oven for 20 minutes. Halfway through the baking, turn the pie around 180 degrees to ensure even cooking. After the pie has cooled, cut it into six slices. Garnish each slice with the whipped cream, a mint leaf, and a lime wheel.

MAKES 1 PIE

Hot Fudge Brownie Sundaes

There are no brownies more luxurious. If you can resist eating them warm from the pan, they are the basis for a seriously chocoholic hot fudge sundae.

FOR THE BROWNIES:

¼ cup unsweetened chocolate

2 cups sugar

½ teaspoon vanilla

¼ cup butter

3 eggs

1 cup cake flour

¾ cup white chocolate chips

¾ cup walnut pieces

FOR THE HOT FUDGE:

4 (1-ounce) squares unsweetened chocolate

½ cup butter

½ teaspoon salt

3 cups sugar

1 (12-ounce) can evaporated milk

½ pint heavy whipping cream

2 tablespoons sugar

Vanilla bean ice cream

Chocolate shavings

6 mint leaves

Preheat the oven to 350°F.

To make the brownies, in a double boiler, melt the unsweetened chocolate. Stir in the sugar until it is well blended. Remove from the heat. With a wooden spatula, stir the vanilla, butter, eggs, cake flour, and white chocolate chips into the mixture. Pour the mixture into a buttered and floured 13 x 9-inch baking pan. Sprinkle the walnuts over the top of the brownies. Bake in the oven for 18 to 22 minutes or until the brownies are mostly cooked through but still soft in the middle. Remove them from the oven. Allow them to cool slightly and cut into 6 squares. Brownies should be served warm.

To make the hot fudge, melt the chocolate, butter, and salt together in the top of a double boiler. Add the sugar, half cup at a time, stirring thoroughly until all the sugar is incorporated into the chocolate. Whisk in the evaporated milk slowly until it is incorporated into the chocolate as well. Remove from the heat.

In a small bowl, whip the whipping cream and the sugar together until it is the desired consistency. Put approximately ¼ cup of hot fudge on the bottom of each plate. Place the brownie on top of the fudge and top with a scoop of vanilla bean ice cream. Garnish with a dollop of whipped cream, chocolate shavings, and a mint leaf.

MAKES 6 SUNDAES

186

Fresh Berries with Zabaglione

Zabaglione is a dessert sauce made by whisking together egg yolks, Marsala, and sugar. The two vital ingredients here are *fresh* sweet berries and good-quality Marsala. If you've got both, you have a glassful of hedonism.

---

8 *cups water*

6 *egg yolks*

4 *tablespoons sugar*

½ *cup Marsala wine*

½ *cup fresh blueberries*

½ *cup fresh blackberries*

½ *cup fresh sliced strawberries*

½ *cup fresh raspberries*

4 *mint sprigs*

In a double boiler or in a medium stainless bowl held over 8 cups simmering water, whisk the egg yolks and sugar together until the mixture becomes frothy. Slowly stir in the Marsala wine. Continue to whisk the mixture until it is very thick and has doubled in volume, 5 to 7 minutes. (This is the zabaglione.) Remove from the heat and continue to beat until the mixture is cooled. Combine the blueberries, blackberries, strawberries, and raspberries and distribute them among four individual parfait glasses. Pour the warm zabaglione over the top of the berries and garnish each parfait glass with a mint sprig. Serve immediately.

MAKES 4 SERVINGS

Cannoli

To make your own cannoli, you need cannelli—the ¾ x 4-inch metal cylinders used as a mold to form the dough into tubular shells to be filled.

FOR THE FILLING:

10   ounces drained ricotta cheese

½   cup superfine sugar

3   ounces finely diced mixed candied fruit

2   tablespoons chopped pistachios

FOR THE DOUGH:

1½   cups flour

¼   cup white wine

½   cup superfine sugar

2   tablespoons honey

½   teaspoon salt

1   egg white

1   egg

FOR THE CANNOLI:

1   egg white

¼   cup canola oil for frying

¼   cup chopped pistachios

¼   cup powdered sugar

To make the filling, combine the ricotta cheese, sugar, candied fruit, and pistachios in a medium bowl. Refrigerate.

To make the dough, in a medium mixing bowl mix together the flour, wine, sugar, honey, salt, egg white, and whole egg. Knead until the mixture is stiff. Wrap the dough in plastic and refrigerate for a minimum of 2 hours.

To make the cannoli, roll out the dough to ⅛-inch thickness and form into approximately 4-inch ovals. Take the cylinders and wrap them with the dough, using the egg white to seal them. In a deep sauté pan, heat the canola oil over high heat to 350°F. Fry the shells in the oil for about 3 to 4 minutes or until they are golden brown on all sides. Drain the shells on paper towels and remove them from the cylinders before the dough has cooled completely. Fill the shells with the ricotta cheese mixture. Dip the ends of the cannoli into the chopped pistachios and then sprinkle them with the powdered sugar. To make chocolate cannoli, add ¼ cup semisweet chocolate chips to the filling mixture. To make chocolate-covered cannoli, melt ½ cup semisweet chocolate chips and dip the ends in the chocolate prior to dipping the ends into the pistachios.

MAKES 10 TO 12 CANNOLI

Carrot Cake with Cream Cheese Frosting

What we like best about the traditional recipe for carrot cake is that its ingredients make enough frosting so that every slice has plenty.

FOR THE CAKE:

1½ cups brown sugar

4 eggs

1 cup vegetable oil

1 teaspoon vanilla

2 cups shredded carrots

½ cup chopped walnuts

½ cup canned diced pineapple chunks

½ cup raisins

2½ cups flour

1 teaspoon cinnamon

1 teaspoon salt

1½ teaspoons baking powder

1½ teaspoons baking soda

FOR THE CREAM CHEESE FROSTING:

1 pound powdered sugar

8 ounces cream cheese

1 teaspoon vanilla

½ cup butter

To make the cake, preheat the oven to 350°F. In a large mixing bowl combine the brown sugar, eggs, oil, vanilla, carrots, walnuts, pineapple, and raisins. In another large bowl combine the flour, cinnamon, salt, baking powder, and baking soda. Slowly stir the flour mixture into the egg mixture, stirring until all the ingredients are incorporated. Divide the mixture evenly between two greased, 12-inch-round baking pans. Bake in the oven for 30 to 40 minutes. Remove from the oven and allow to cool.

To make the cream cheese frosting, combine the powdered sugar, cream cheese, vanilla, and butter in a large bowl. Stir until the mixture is smooth and creamy. Even off the top of one of the cakes to make the bottom layer of the cake. Frost the top of this (bottom) layer. Place the second layer on top and frost the entire cake.

MAKES 1 CAKE

Lemon Cheesecake

We're not sure how cheesecake became the conventional dessert after a big steak meal. In this case, the lemon twist does give it a nice refreshing flavor . . . even if it is rich as sin.

FOR THE CRUST:

1½   cups graham cracker crumbs

⅓   cup melted butter

⅓   cup sugar

FOR THE FILLING:

24   ounces cream cheese

1   cup sugar

4   eggs

2   teaspoons grated lemon zest

3   tablespoons lemon juice

2   teaspoons Grand Marnier

1   cup sour cream

Preheat the oven to 350°F. To make the crust, combine the graham cracker crumbs, melted butter, and sugar in a medium bowl. Press the crust into the bottom of an 8-inch springform pan.

To make the filling, combine the cream cheese and sugar in a large mixing bowl and whisk, or use a hand mixer, until the mixture is very smooth. Add the eggs one at a time, beating until the mixture is smooth again. Add the lemon zest, lemon juice, and Grand Marnier. Fold in the sour cream and mix just until blended. Pour the filling into the springform pan. Place the pan into a larger pan and surround it with 1 inch of hot water. Bake the cheesecake in the hot water bath for 60 to 90 minutes. Remove the cake from the oven and allow it to cool for at least 1 hour before removing it from the springform pan.

MAKES 1 CHEESECAKE

Chocolate Chip Cheesecake

Looking for a way to have your cheesecake and eat chocolate, too? There are some of us for whom no dessert is fully satisfying unless it pays homage to the cocoa bean.

FOR THE CRUST:

1½ cups ground Oreo cookie crumbs

⅓ cup melted butter

FOR THE FILLING:

24 ounces cream cheese

1 cup sugar

3 eggs

2 teaspoons vanilla

1½ cups semisweet chocolate chips

1 cup sour cream

To make the crust, preheat the oven to 325°F. In a medium mixing bowl, combine the cookie crumbs and melted butter. Press the crust into the bottom of an 8-inch springform pan.

To make the filling, in a large mixing bowl combine the cream cheese and sugar and whisk or use a hand mixer until the mixture is very smooth. Add the eggs one at a time, beating until the mixture is smooth again. Add the vanilla and chocolate chips. Fold in the sour cream and mix just until blended. Pour the filling into the springform pan. Place the pan into a larger pan and surround it with 1 inch of hot water. Bake in the hot water bath for 60 to 90 minutes. Remove the cake from the oven and allow it to cool for at least 1 hour before removing it from the springform pan.

MAKES 1 CHEESECAKE

Chocolate Tortas with Warm Caramel Pecan Sauce

Chicago isn't the only place that has a fondness for the combination of chocolate and caramel—known throughout the Midwest as "turtle" flavor (as in turtles candy). No city has more and better opportunities to savor it. Here is Harry Caray's super luxury rendition.

FOR THE TORTA SHELLS:

2½ sticks plus 1 tablespoon butter at room temperature

½ cup plus 1½ tablespoons powdered sugar

½ cup finely ground almonds

½ teaspoon salt

3 eggs

½ cup cocoa powder

2¾ cups flour

FOR THE CARAMEL PECAN SAUCE:

1 pint heavy whipping cream

1¾ cups sugar

1¾ cups lightly toasted pecan halves

Vanilla bean ice cream

1 pint blackberries

Mint sprigs

FOR THE TORTA FILLING (CHOCOLATE CREAM GANACHE):

1 pound superfine dark chocolate pieces

8 tablespoons butter at room temperature

2 cups heavy cream

The torta shells should be made a day in advance.

To make the torta shells, use a hand mixer on slow speed and in a large mixing bowl beat all the butter until it is creamy and smooth. Slowly add all the powdered sugar, ground almonds, salt, and eggs. Scrape the sides of the bowl with a spatula and continue to mix on slow speed. Add the cocoa powder until it is evenly combined with the mixture. Add the flour ½ cup at a time until it is evenly combined with the mixture to make a soft dough. Separate the dough into three even balls, wrap them with plastic, and refrigerate overnight.

To make the torta filling, place the chocolate pieces in a large mixing bowl. Place the butter in a medium bowl and mash it with a spatula until it is creamy. In a small saucepan bring the heavy cream to a boil and then remove it from the heat. Slowly add the heavy cream a bit at a time to the chocolate pieces and mix with a spatula until the cream is thoroughly incorporated into the chocolate. Add the butter to the chocolate mixture a small amount at a time until it is thoroughly incorporated into the chocolate mixture as well. If the mixture gets too cold to blend, place the bowl with the chocolate mixture over a pan of simmering water and blend.

To make the caramel pecan sauce, heat the whipping cream over medium heat until the cream begins to bubble and then remove it from the heat. In a heavy-bottomed saucepan, heat the sugar over a low flame. Stir constantly so the sugar does not burn. Melt the sugar until it is a light brown color. Carefully add the heavy cream to the sugar, a small bit at a time. It is normal for the cream to splatter. When all the heavy cream is incorporated into the sugar, stir in the pecans. Remove from the heat and keep warm until serving.

To assemble the tortas, remove the dough from the refrigerator and allow it to come to room temperature. Preheat the oven to 350°F. Divide each ball into four equal pieces and roll them to ⅛-inch-thick circles. Lightly press each piece of dough into a 3-inch tart pan and cut the excess dough from around the edges. Cover the bottom of each tart with a circle of wax paper, and fill the tart with dry beans to weigh down the dough. Place the tarts on a cookie sheet and bake for 10 minutes. Remove from the oven and allow to cool. Remove the beans and the wax paper and fill each torta with the warm chocolate ganache and refrigerate for a least 1 hour.

To serve, place the tortas on individual plates in the center of the plate. Ladle a 3-ounce portion of the warm caramel pecan sauce over the top of the torta. Top with a scoop of vanilla bean ice cream and garnish with fresh blackberries and a mint sprig.

MAKES 12 TORTAS

Crème Brûlée

Literally meaning "burnt cream," this velvet-smooth dessert may require a bit of pyrotechnical derring-do. If you don't have a totally predictable, even-temperature broiler, use a hand-held browning tool (a small butane torch). You need it to create the characteristic brittle top with its caramelized-verging-on-burnt flavor.

5	cups heavy whipping cream
½	vanilla bean (or 2 teaspoons vanilla extract)
½	plus ½ cup sugar
2	tablespoons Grand Marnier
1¼	cups egg yolk
2	tablespoons sugar
	Powdered sugar
1	pint assorted fresh berries
	Mint sprigs

Preheat the oven to 325°F. In a medium saucepan combine the heavy whipping cream, vanilla bean, ½ cup sugar, and Grand Marnier. In a medium mixing bowl, combine the egg yolks and the remaining ½ cup sugar. Whisk the egg yolk mixture together until thoroughly combined. Heat the whipping cream mixture over medium heat until bubbles form at the edge of the pot. Whisk ½ cup of the whipping cream mixture into the egg yolk mixture. Now whisk the egg mixture into the remaining whipping cream mixture. Whisk constantly until the mixture thickens enough to coat the back of a spoon. Immediately strain the mixture into a medium bowl. Pour into individual crème brûlée baking dishes, filling each dish three-fourths full. Place the baking dishes into a larger dish and fill the bottom dish with 1 inch of hot water. Bake in the oven for 45 minutes. Remove from the oven and allow the crème brûlée to cool. Lightly sprinkle the top of each crème brûlée with sugar. Before serving, evenly brown the top of the crème brûlée with a butane torch until it forms a sugar crust. Place the crème brûlée dish on a large plate and garnish with powdered sugar and fresh berries around the edge of the plate. Place a mint sprig on the crème brûlée and serve.

MAKES 12 SERVINGS

Crème Anglaise

Whipped cream isn't rich enough for you? Crème Anglaise (English cream) is the answer: whipped cream made thicker and creamier by cooking with egg yolks.

2	*cups heavy cream*
1	*tablespoon vanilla*
¾	*cup egg yolks*
¾	*cup sugar*

In a heavy-bottomed saucepan heat the heavy cream and vanilla until bubbles form at the edge of the pot. While the cream is heating, whisk together the egg yolks and the sugar in a small bowl until the mixture is smooth. Pour half of the heavy cream mixture into the egg mixture, whisking constantly. Gradually add the egg yolk mixture back into the saucepan containing the heavy cream mixture, whisking constantly until the mixture is thick enough to coat the back of a spoon. Remove the Crème Anglaise from the heat, pour it into a medium mixing bowl, and immediately chill it in an ice bath to stop the cooking process. Use the Crème Anglaise as a hot or cold topping over fresh fruit, cake, or other dessert.

MAKES 3 CUPS

Mini Warm Apple Pies with Apple Cinnamon Ice Cream

We love Chicago in the fall, because it is a city that appreciates autumn apples. Freshly picked ones from Michigan appear in markets; and street corner candy stores dip them in caramel to make fresh caramel apples. These mini pies à la mode are Harry Caray's year-round celebration of apples.

FOR THE DOUGH:

2   sticks unsalted butter, softened

2¼ cups flour

¼   teaspoon salt
    Cold water

FOR THE FILLING:

¼   pound butter

6   Granny Smith apples, peeled, cored, and
    diced

¼   teaspoon nutmeg

1½ teaspoons ground cinnamon

6   tablespoons granulated sugar

6   tablespoons brown sugar

3   teaspoons cornstarch

3   teaspoons water

1   egg white
    Apple cinnamon or vanilla ice cream

To make the dough, knead the butter, flour, and salt together in a medium mixing bowl. Slowly add cold water until the dough comes together. Cover the dough with plastic wrap and refrigerate for a minimum of 1 hour.

For the apple filling, heat the butter in a medium sauté pan over medium-high heat. Add the apples and sauté for 1 minute. Season with the nutmeg and cinnamon. Sauté the mixture for 1 more minute. Add the sugar and brown sugar and stir until all the lumps are gone. In a small bowl, combine the cornstarch and water. Add the cornstarch mixture to the sauté pan and sauté for 3 more minutes. Transfer the apple mixture to a cookie sheet and refrigerate.

To assemble the pies, separate the dough into six equal parts. Preheat the oven to 350°F. Flour each piece and roll it into a circle ⅛-inch thick. Place the dough into six individual, 4½-inch springform pans. Fill each pan halfway with the apple mixture and fold the edges of the dough over into the pie. Brush the top with egg whites and bake for 15 minutes or until the pies begin to bubble. Let the pies cool, remove them from the pans, and serve them with apple cinnamon ice cream.

MAKES 6 MINI PIES

Glossary

Aglio e Olio – Any pasta tossed with olive oil and garlic.

Al Dente – Literally, "to the tooth," referring to pasta cooked so it still has a slightly chewy nature.

Antipasto – Literally "before the food". Usually an assortment of hot and cold Italian appetizers.

Arborio Rice – Short, chubby rice kernels with extra starch content, usually used for risotto.

Arugula – A bitter salad green with mustard flavor.

Asiago – A rich semifirm cheese with a nutty flavor. It can be made from whole or part-skim cow's milk.

Balsamic Vinegar – Made from trebbiano grapes and aged in barrels for a number of years. This vinegar has a distinctive, tangy/sweet flavor quite different from standard vinegars.

Blanched – To partially cook food in boiling water. Blanching brings out the color in green vegetables and helps loosen skins on fruit.

Braise – A cooking method that gets maximum flavor from food. Braising means to brown meat in fat, partially cover it with liquid, then cook tightly covered over low heat.

Bruschetta – Toasted garlic bread that often comes with various toppings, such as roasted peppers or tomatoes.

Cannellini Beans – White Italian kidney beans, used in salads and hot dishes.

Coppa – The name of both a cut of pork and a cured meat obtained from the upper part of the neck and the shoulder of pork, mostly prepared in central and southern Italy. Meat and fat are cut into large chunks and flavored with different spices in different regions, and cured for four months to one year. The cured meat is thinly sliced and eaten raw in delightful antipasto platters.

Cappellini – Slightly thicker than angel hair pasta but still very thin, long strands.

Carbonara – A pasta dish that features bacon, eggs and cream.

Chanterelle – A delicate-flavored mushroom with a flavor often described as fruity.

Ciabatta – Literally, "slipper," referring to the flat oval shape of a bread loaf.

Clarified Butter – Slowly-melted butter in which water and milk solids are separated. With the milk solids removed, it can be used to cook food at a higher temperature because it burns less quickly.

Cremini – Firm, full-flavored mushrooms with rounded caps.

Deglaze – To deglaze a pan is to pour in a small amount of liquid (wine or stock) after cooking meat and stirring it with the bits of food stuck to the bottom. This is usually the basis for sauce or gravy.

Escarole – A broad form of endive that has curly, pale green leaves. It has a slight bitter taste.

Farfalle – Bow-tie shaped pasta. Name translates to "butterflies".

Focaccia – Baked flatbread that is liberally brushed with olive oil and sprinkled with salt. A lot of times it is seasoned with rosemary.

Fontina – A semifirm yet creamy, high-fat cheese that has a nutty flavor.

French – 1) To cut vegetables or meat lengthwise into thin strips. 2) To cut the meat away from the end of a rib or chop to expose the bone.

Frisée – A delicate kind of chicory with a mild flavor.

Fusilli – Corkscrew-shaped pasta made with semolina, flour, and water. The name derives from the word fuso which means "twisted", due to its spiral shape. Fusilli are usually served with tomato or meat-based sauces.

Genoa Salami – A rich, fatty Italian pork salami studded with white peppercorns.

Gnocchi – Small dumplings, usually made from potatoes.

Goat Cheese – Called chèvre, it's a pure white goat's-milk cheese with a tart flavor.

Gorgonzola – Named for a town outside of Milan, this is a pungent veined cheese often used in salads.

Gruyère – A Swiss cheese with a sweet, nutty flavor.

Marsala – Italy's most famous fortified wine. It has a rich, smoky flavor and comes in various styles: *secco* (dry), *semisecco* (semisweet), and *dolce* (sweet).

Mascarpone – Ivory white double-cream or triple-cream cheese often used in desserts.

Mesclun Greens – A mix of young, small, delicate salad greens, including iceberg, green leaf lettuce, romaine, radicchio, and mesclun greens.

Mortadella – Made from 60% lean pork and 40% pork fat, Mortadella is a delicious cured meat that has origins in the Emilian city of Bologna. The pork meat is stuffed into a casing, shaped into a long, fat cylinder, and studded with peppercorns or pistachios. Savor Mortadella thinly sliced in sandwiches or cubed in meatballs or pasta sauces.

Orecchiette – Ear-shaped pasta translates to "ears". Their indentation makes them ideal for rich sauces.

Osso Buco – One of Italy's favorite dishes, osso buco is made of braised veal shanks. The meat is first browned, then cooked with vegetables and aromatic herbs until they are extremely tender and the meat falls off the bones. The marrow is the most delicious and prized part, it can be scooped out with a teaspoon.

Pancetta – The section taken from the fat belly or cheek of a pig, consisting of alternating layers of fat and lean tissue. It can be rolled, aged, salted or smoked. It is basically Italian un-smoked bacon.

Panko – Coarse bread crumbs used in coating fried foods. They are predominantly used in Japanese cooking and create a crunchy crust.

Parmigiana – Any food cooked with Parmesan cheese.

Parmigiano-Reggiano – A hard, dry cheese that is made from skimmed cow's milk. Parmigiano-Reggiano is made in Italy and aged for around two years as compared to American or Australian Parmesan cheeses, which are typically aged for 14 months.

Pecorino Romano – A hard, granular, and sharp Italian cheese made of sheep's milk. It is the best known of the pecorino cheeses.

Penne – Medium length pasta tubes with ends cut on an angle. Can be ridged.

Pepperoncini – Thin, two- to three-inch long chiles that have a bright red, wrinkled skin with a slightly sweet flavor. They're usually pickled and used in an antipasto.

Polenta – A mush made from cornmeal and a staple of northern Italy. It is eaten hot with butter or when cooled it is cut into squares and fried.

Porcini – Also called *cèpes,* these are wild pale brown mushrooms with a smooth, meaty texture and pungent, woodsy flavor.

Portobello – An extremely large, dark brown mushroom with an enriched flavor and a dense, meaty texture.

Prosciutto – Prosciutto is a cured ham. It is taken from the hind thigh of a pig. All types of prosciutto are cured in a similar way, but the curing time varies from 9 to 18 months, the average being 14 months. The meat is kept in cold store rooms to harden and then it is pressed and cleaned, and stripped of excess fat. It is then salted, brushed, cleaned and rested before it goes through the aging process. Prosciutto can be sliced paper-thin and served in sandwiches, on top of salads or pizzas, or diced in pasta sauces.

Radicchio – A red-leafed Italian chicory (endive) that is used as a salad green.

Reduce – To reduce volume of a liquid by boiling it in a pot so that a portion evaporates.

Ricotta – A rich fresh cheese that is smoother than cottage cheese with a slightly sweet flavor. Most Italian ricottas are made from the whey that is drained when making other cheeses.

Ricotta Salata – A variation of ricotta, this firm rindless sheep's milk cheese originated in Sicily. It is mild and nutty and ideal for grating.

Rigatoni – Fat, squat pasta tubes with a grooved exterior.

Risotto – Italian rice dish that is prepared by slowly adding a stock to the grain. It can be served with many ingredients, such as sausage or chicken.

Romano – Named for the city of Rome, most U.S. Romanos are made of cow's milk or a combination of cow's milk and goat's or sheep's milk. The pale yellow cheese is very firm and used mostly for grating.

Rotini – A short spiral pasta that is about one to two inches long.

Roux – A mixture of flour and fat cooked over low heat that is used to thicken soups and sauces. White roux is made with butter and brown roux is usually made with drippings.

Saffron – The world's most expensive spice, it comes in stigmas or a powdered form. This pungent, aromatic spice goes a long way in flavoring and tinting food.

Shiitake – Originally from Japan and Korea, this dark brown mushroom has meaty flesh with a steaklike flavor.

Soppressata – Soppressata is type of salami made in central Italy. It is made with lean pork meat from the shoulder, mixed with fatty ground pancetta, cut into sticks and packed into natural casing, which is washed in wine vinegar. It has a soft consistency and a delicate smoky flavor.

Stock – Strained liquid after cooking vegetables, meat or fish, and seasonings in water.

Tagliatelle – Long, flat strands of pasta that are slightly wider than fettuccine.

Tubetti – Literally, "little tubes," these pastas are tiny, hollow tubes.

Zabaglione – This luscious dessert is made by whisking egg yolks with sugar and dry Marsala wine in a double boiler until a rich cream forms. Variations include the use of other sweet wines like Moscato, Vin Santo, Prosecco, and port.

Zest – The perfumy outermost skin layer of citrus fruit, not the white pith, which is removed with a zester, grater, or paring knife.

Ziti – Narrow pasta tubes of medium length. Similar to Penne except ends are not cut on an angle.

Index

A

Aaron, Hank, 74

Ahi, *See* tuna

Alfredo Sauce, 83

antipasto

Antipasto Platter, 58

Antipasto Salad, 25

appetizers

Antipasto Platter, 58

Asparagus with Prosciutto and
Gorgonzola in Peppercorn
Vinaigrette, 63

Baked Clams, 55

Beef Carpaccio with Porcini
Mushrooms and Roasted Red
Pepper Relish, 65

Grilled Marinated Octopus with
Spicy Infused Olive Oil, 51

Harry's Bruschetta, 49

Jumbo Lump Crab Cakes, 52

Jumbo Shrimp Cocktail, 53

Mozzarella Marinara, 59

Mussels Marinara, 60

Mussels Steamed in Garlic, 61

Prosciutto and Melon, 64

Roasted Red Peppers, 54

Savory Italian Cheese Platter, 50

Shrimp Marsala, 62

Sweet Italian Cheese Platter, 66

Apple pie, apple cinnamon ice cream
with, 146

Arrabbiata Sauce, 84

Arugula, risotto with, 125

asparagus

Asparagus with Prosciutto and
Gorgonzola in Peppercorn
Vinaigrette, 63

Grilled Asparagus, 78

Saffron Risotto with Cremini
Mushrooms, Asparagus, and
Grilled Sea Scallops, 121

Aurore Sauce, 86

B

Baked Clams, 55

Baked Grouper Oreganato, 141

Baked Salmon with Olives, 139

Baked Ziti, 107

Banks, Ernie, 74, 75

Baseball Hall of Fame, 74, 75

Basic Risotto, 118

Baylor, Don, 75

beef

Beef Carpaccio with Porcini
Mushrooms and Roasted Red
Pepper Relish, 65

Beef Filet Wrapped in
Pancetta, 167

Beef Tenderloin Tips with
Gorgonzola Cheese and Roma
Tomatoes, 182

Bone-In Rib-Eye Steak, 168

Filet Mignon Served over
Barolo Risotto with Parmesan
Crisps, 122

Grilled New York Strip Sirloin
Sandwiches, 44

Harry's Signature New York Strip,
Peppercorn Style, 163

Homemade Beef Stock, 95

Homemade Italian Meatballs, 69

Italian Beef Sandwiches
Au Jus, 37

Italian Meatball Sandwiches, 46

Italian Steak Pizziola, 166

Marco Polo, 131

Meat Lasagna, 109

Meat Sauce, 82

Pepper-Crusted Beef Medallion
Sandwiches, 45

Spaghetti with Italian
Meatballs, 110

Surf and Turf, 181

Bordelaise Sauce, 93

Braised Chicken with Kalamata
Olives and Fresh Sage, 160

Brandy Shallot Butter, 90

broccoli

Broccoli Salad, 32

Grilled Halibut Fillet with Broccoli
and Chanterelle Mushroom
Risotto, 120

Sautéed Broccoli and Mushrooms
with Garlic, 76

Broiled Australian Cold-Water Rock
Lobster Tails, 146

Bone-In Rib-Eye Steak, 168

Brownie sundaes, hot fudge, 186

Bruschetta, 49

Budweiser beer, 1, 2, 40–41, 75, 151

butter

Brandy Shallot Butter, 90

Clarified Butter, 90

Pan-Seared, Peppered Yellowfin
Tuna with Pinot Grigio Butter
Sauce, 137

C

Caesar Salad, 22

cakes

Carrot Cake with Cream Cheese
Frosting, 189

203

cakes *continued*
   Chocolate Chip Cheesecake, 191
   Lemon Cheescake, 190
Cannoli, 188
Capellini, shrimp scampi over, 113
Capone, Al, 15, 92
Carabina, Harry Christopher, 3,
   154, 172
Caray, Chip, 75, 159
Caray, Dutchie, 2–3, 4, 16, 31, 172
Caray, Harry, 1–4, 16, 17, 18, 31, 40,
   41, 74, 75, 98, 163, 172, 173
Caray, Skip, 159
Carbonara, linguine with, 105
Carrot Cake with Cream Cheese
   Frosting, 189
cheese
   Asparagus with Prosciutto and
     Gorgonzola in Peppercorn
     Vinaigrette, 63
   Beef Tenderloin Tips with
     Gorgonzola Cheese and Roma
     Tomatoes, 182
   Chicken Parmigiana, 156
   Chicken Parmigiana
     Sandwiches, 38
   Eggplant Parmigiana, 130
   Filet Mignon Served over
     Barolo Risotto with Parmesan
     Crisps, 122
   Linguine with Lemon-Garlic
     Shrimp and Parmigiano-Reggiano
     Cream Sauce, 116–117
   Mozzarella Marinara, 59
   Risotto with Pancetta, Arugula, and
     Goat Cheese, 125
   Savory Italian Cheese Platter, 50
   Sweet Italian Cheese Platter, 66
   Veal Parmigiana, 169
cheesecakes
   Chocolate Chip Cheesecake, 191
   Lemon Cheesecake, 190
Chicago Cubs, xiii, 1, 2, 40, 41, 74, 75, 151
Chicago White Sox, 1, 2, 3, 31, 40, 74, 75
chicken
   Braised Chicken with Kalamata
     Olives and Fresh Sage, 160

Chicken Cacciatore, 153
Chicken Carabina, 154
Chicken Italiano, 159
Chicken Limone, 155
Chicken Marsala, 157
Chicken Milanese, 152
Chicken Parmigiana, 156
Chicken Parmigiana
   Sandwiches, 38
Chicken Piccata, 158
Chicken Vesuvio Salad, 23
Chicken Vesuvio Sandwiches, 43
Chopped Salad with Chicken, 21
Harry's Signature Chicken Vesuvio
   (Bone-In), 149
Harry's Signature Chicken Vesuvio
   (Boneless Breast), 150
Homemade Chicken Stock, 94
Marco Polo, 131
Pesto Chicken Pasta Salad, 24
Risotto with Oven-Roasted
   Chicken, Caramelized
   Onions, and Portabella
   Mushrooms, 124
Ziti with Grilled Chicken and Pesto
   Sauce, 108
Chilled Lobster Salad with Garlic Toast
   Points, 33
Chocolate Chip Cheesecake, 191
Chocolate Tortas with Warm Caramel
   Pecan Sauce, 192–93
Chopped Salad with Chicken, 21
clams
   Baked Clams, 55
   Linguine di Mare, 112
   Linguine with Red Clam Sauce, 115
   Linguine with White Clam Sauce, 114
Clarified Butter, 90
Cobb, Henry Ives, 15
Cocktail Sauce, 89
Comiskey Park, 1, 18, 31, 74, 75
Costas, Bob, 16
Crab cakes, 52
Cream of Zucchini Soup, 11
Creamed Spinach, 77
Creamy Potato and Pancetta Soup, 14
Creamy Roasted Garlic Soup, 10

Crème Anglaise, 195
Crème Brûlée, 194

D
Daley, Richard M., 74
DePorter, Grant, 1, 16–17, 41, 172
desserts
   Cannoli, 188
   Carrot Cake with Cream Cheese
     Frosting, 189
   Chocolate Chip Cheesecake, 191
   Chocolate Tortas with Warm
     Caramel Pecan Sauce, 192–93
   Crème Anglaise, 195
   Crème Brûlée, 194
   Fresh Berries with Zabaglione, 187
   Hot Fudge Brownie Sundaes, 186
   Key Lime Pie, 185
   Lemon Cheesecake, 190
   Mini Warm Apple Pies with Apple
     Cinnamon Ice Cream, 196
Dickie, Garrick, xi, 56, 57, 140
dressings
   Harry's Caesar Dressing, 99
   Italian Vinaigrette, 100
   Raspberry Vinaigrette, 98
   Sun-Dried Tomato Vinaigrette, 96
   Sweet Herb Vinaigrette, 97
dumplings
   Homemade Gnocchi with Roasted
     Red Peppers and Mushrooms, 133
Dutchie's Salad, 30

E
Eggplant Parmigiana, 130

F
feature stories
   beef, 164–65
   Chicago Way to Eat, the, 56–57
   Cub Fan Bud Man, 40–41
   Dutchie, 31
   45¢ Beer, 151
   Frenk Nitti, 92
   Harry Caray, 1–4
   Memorabilia on Display, 74–75
   Seafood at Harry's, 140

feature stories *continued*
    Thanksgiving for Orphans,
        172–73
    33 West Kenzie Street, 15–18
Fennel, rotini with, 104
Fettucini Alfredo Primavera, 106
Filet Mignon Served over Barolo Risotto
    with Parmesan Crisps, 122
Fish, *See* seafood
Fresh Berries with Zabaglione, 187
Fried Shrimp, 145
Frosting, cream cheese, 189
fruit
    Fresh Berries with Zabaglione, 187
    Prosciutto and Melon, 64

G
garlic
    Chilled Lobster Salad with Garlic
        Toast Points, 33
    Creamy Roasted Garlic Soup, 10
    Garlic Mashed Potatoes, 71
    Mussels Steamed in Garlic, 61
    Pasta with Aglio Olio Sauce (Garlic
        and Olive Oil), 111
    Sautéed Broccoli and Mushrooms
        with Garlic, 76
    Sautéed Spinach with Garlic
        and Oil, 70
Gnocchi with roasted red peppers and
    mushrooms, 133
Goldmann, Dolores, 31
    See also Caray, Dutchie
Gorgonzola
    Asparagus with Prosciutto and
        Gorgonzola in Peppercorn
        Vinaigrette, 63
    Beef Tenderloin Tips with
        Gorgonzola Cheese and Roma
        Tomatoes, 182
    Great Tomato, Onion, and Anchovy
        Salad, 29
    Grilled Asparagus, 78
    Grilled Halibut Fillet with Broccoli and
        Chanterelle Mushroom Risotto, 120
    Grilled Marinated Octopus with Spicy
        Infused Olive Oil, 51

Grilled New York Strip Sirloin
    Sandwiches, 44
Grilled Pork Chops with Applesauce, 178
Grilled Yellowfin Tuna (Ahi)
    Sandwiches, 39
Grouper, baked with oreganato, 141

H
Halibut fillet, grilled, 120
Harry Caray's Italian Steakhouse, 18
Harry Caray's Walk of Fame, 18
Harry's Bruschetta, 49
Harry's Caesar Dressing, 99
Harry's Signature Chicken Vesuvio
    (Bone-In), 149
Harry's Signature Chicken Vesuvio
    (Boneless Breast), 150
Harry's Signature New York Strip,
    Peppercorn Style, 163
Heller, Beth Goldberg, 16
Hollandaise Sauce, 91
holy cow, 75, 164
Holy Cow! potato chips, xiii
Homemade Beef Stock, 95
Homemade Chicken Stock, 94
Homemade Gnocchi with Roasted Red
    Peppers and Mushrooms, 133
Homemade Italian Meatballs, 69
Hot Fudge Brownie Sundaes, 186

I
Italian Beef Sandwiches Au Jus, 37
Italian Meatball Sandwiches, 46
Italian Onion Soup, 9
Italian Sausage and Peppers, 129
Italian Steak Pizziola, 166
Italian-Style Salmon, 144
Italian Vinaigrette, 100

J
Jumbo Lump Crab Cakes, 52
Jumbo Shrimp Cocktail, 53

K
Key Lime Pie, 185
Key West Key Lime Shop, 185

L
lamb
    Lamb Chops with Mint Jelly, 177
    Lamb Chops Oreganato, 176
leeks
    Plum-Glazed Salmon with Polenta
        and Fried Leeks, 142–43
    Risotto with Italian Sausage and
        Leeks, 126
Lemon Cheesecake, 190
Levy, Marv, 16, 172
linguine
    Linguine Carbonara, 105
    Linguine with Lemon-Garlic
        Shrimp and Parmigiano-Reggiano
        Cream Sauce, 116–17
    Linguine di Mare, 112
    Linguine with Red Clam Sauce, 115
    Linguine with White Clam Sauce, 114
lobster
    Broiled Australian Cold-Water
        Rock Lobster Tails, 146
    Chilled Lobster Salad with Garlic
        Toast Points, 33
    Surf and Turf, 181

M
Marco Polo, 131
marinara
    Marinara Sauce, 81
    Mozzarella Marinara, 59
    Mussels Marinara, 60
Marsala
    Chicken Marsala, 157
    Shrimp Marsala, 62
    Veal Marsala, 174
Maryville Youth Academy, 31, 172–73
McGwire, Mark, 41
Meat Lasagna, 109
Meat Sauce, 82
meatballs
    Homemade Italian Meatballs, 69
    Italian Meatball Sandwiches, 46
    Spaghetti with Italian
        Meatballs, 110
Melon, prosciutto with, 64
Minestrone Soup, 7

Mini Warm Apple Pies with Apple
  Cinnamon Ice Cream, 196
Mixed Green Salad, 26
Mozzarella Marinara, 59
mushrooms
  Beef Carpaccio with Porcini
    Mushrooms and Roasted Red
    Pepper Relish, 65
  Grilled Halibut Fillet with Broccoli and
    Chanterelle Mushroom Risotto, 120
  Homemade Gnocchi with
    Roasted Red Peppers and
    Mushrooms, 133
  Risotto with Oven-Roasted
    Chicken, Caramelized Onions,
    and Portabella Mushrooms, 124
  Rotini with Italian Sausage,
    Fennel, and Portobello
    Mushrooms, 104
  Saffron Risotto with Cremini
    Mushrooms, Asparagus, and
    Grilled Sea Scallops, 121
  Sautéed Broccoli and Mushrooms
    with Garlic, 76
  Sautéed Mushrooms, 73
  Sweet Potato and Wild Mushroom
    Risotto, 119
Musial, Stan, 74
mussels
  Linguine di Mare, 112
  Mussels Marinara, 60
  Mussels Steamed in Garlic, 61

N
Nitti, Frank "the Enforcer," 15, 92

O
Oakland A's, 2, 74
octopus
  Grilled Marinated Octopus with
    Spicy Infused Olive Oil, 51
  Linguine di Mare, 112
olives
  Baked Salmon with Olives, 139
  Braised Chicken with Kalamata
    Olives and Fresh Sage, 160

onions
  Brandy Shallot Butter, 90
  Great Tomato, Onion, and Anchovy
    Salad, 29
  Italian Onion Soup, 9
  Potato and Onion Soup, 13
  Risotto with Oven-Roasted
    Chicken, Caramelized Onions,
    and Portabella Mushrooms, 124
  Veal Chops with Peppers and
    Onions, 175
Osso Buco, 132

P
Pan-Seared, Peppered Yellowfin Tuna
  with Pinot Grigio Butter Sauce, 137
pancetta
  Beef Fillet Wrapped in Pancetta, 167
  Creamy Potato and Pancetta
    Soup, 14
  Linguine Carbonara, 105
  Risotto with Pancetta, Arugula, and
    Goat Cheese, 125
Panzanella (Tuscan Bread Salad), 28
Parmesan
  Filet Mignon Served over Barolo
    Risotto with Parmesan Crisps, 122
  See also parmigiana
parmigiana
  Chicken Parmigiana, 156
  Chicken Parmigiana Sandwiches, 38
  Eggplant Parmigiana, 130
  Veal Parmigiana, 169
pasta
  Baked Ziti, 107
  Fettucini Alfredo Primavera, 106
  Linguine Carbonara, 105
  Linguine with Lemon-Garlic
    Shrimp and Parmigiano-Reggiano
    Cream Sauce, 116–17
  Linguine di Mare, 112
  Linguine with Red Clam Sauce, 115
  Linguine with White Clam Sauce, 114
  Meat Lasagna, 109
  Pasta with Aglio Olio Sauce (Garlic
    and Olive Oil), 111
  Pesto Chicken Pasta Salad, 24

Rigatoni with Vodka Sauce, 103
Rotini with Italian Sausage,
  Fennel, and Portobello
  Mushrooms, 104
Rotini Pasta Salad, 34
Shrimp Scampi over Capellini, 113
Spaghetti with Italian Meatballs, 110
Ziti with Grilled Chicken and Pesto
  Sauce, 108
Pepper-Crusted Beef Medallion
  Sandwiches, 45
peppercorn
  Asparagus with Prosciutto and
    Gorgonzola in Peppercorn
    Vinaigrette, 63
  Harry's Signature New York Strip,
    Peppercorn Style, 163
peppers
  Beef Carpaccio with Porcini
    Mushrooms and Roasted Red
    Pepper Relish, 65
  Homemade Gnocchi with Roasted
    Red Peppers and Mushrooms, 133
  Italian Sausage and Peppers, 129
  Roasted Red Pepper Cream Sauce, 88
  Roasted Red Peppers, 54
  Stuffed Sweet Red Peppers, 134
  Veal Chops with Peppers and
    Onions, 175
pesto
  Pesto Chicken Pasta Salad, 24
  Pesto Sauce, 85
pies
  Key Lime Pie, 185
  Mini Warm Apple Pies with Apple
    Cinnamon Ice Cream, 196
Plum-Glazed Salmon with Polenta and
  Fried Leeks, 142–43
Polenta, plum-glazed salmon with,
  142–43
pork
  Antipasto Platter, 58
  Creamy Potato and Pancetta Soup, 14
  Grilled Pork Chops with
    Applesauce, 178
  Homemade Italian Meatballs, 69
  Italian Meatball Sandwiches, 46

pork *continued*
  Meat Sauce, 82
  Pork Chops, Italian Style, 179
  Spaghetti with Italian Meatballs, 110
  Stuffed Italian Pork Chops, 180
potatoes
  Creamy Potato and Pancetta Soup, 14
  Garlic Mashed Potatoes, 71
  Potato and Onion Soup, 13
  potato chips, xiii
  Sweet Potato and Wild Mushroom
    Risotto, 119
  Vesuvio Potatoes, 72
prosciutto
  Asparagus with Prosciutto and
    Gorgonzola in Peppercorn
    Vinaigrette, 63
  Prosciutto and Melon, 64

R
Raspberry Vinaigrette, 98
relish
  Beef Carpaccio with Porcini
    Mushrooms and Roasted Red
    Pepper Relish, 65
Rémoulade Sauce, 87
Rice, *See* Risotto
Rigatoni with Vodka Sauce, 103
risotto
  Basic Risotto, 118
  Filet Mignon Served over
    Barolo Risotto with Parmesan
    Crisps, 122
  Grilled Halibut Fillet with Broccoli
    and Chanterelle Mushroom
    Risotto, 120
  Risotto with Italian Sausage and
    Leeks, 126
  Risotto with Oven-Roasted
    Chicken, Caramelized Onions,
    and Portobello Mushrooms, 124
  Risotto with Pancetta, Arugula, and
    Goat Cheese, 125
  Roasted Vegetable Risotto, 123
  Saffron Risotto with Cremini
    Mushrooms, Asparagus, and
    Grilled Sea Scallops, 121

Sweet Potato and Wild Mushroom
  Risotto, 119
River North, 15
Roasted Red Pepper Cream Sauce, 88
Roasted Red Peppers, 54
Roasted Turkey Club Sandwiches, 42
Roasted Vegetable Risotto, 123
rotini
  Rotini Pasta Salad, 34
  Rotini with Italian Sausage, Fennel,
    and Portobello Mushrooms, 104

S
Saffron Risotto with Cremini
  Mushrooms, Asparagus, and
  Grilled Sea Scallops, 121
Sage, chicken with, 160
salads
  Antipasto Salad, 25
  Broccoli Salad, 32
  Caesar Salad, 22
  Chicken Vesuvio Salad, 23
  Chilled Lobster Salad with Garlic
    Toast Points, 33
  Chopped Salad with Chicken, 21
  Dutchie's Salad, 30
  Great Tomato, Onion, and Anchovy
    Salad, 29
  Mixed Green Salad, 26
  Panzanella (Tuscan Bread
    Salad), 28
  Pesto Chicken Pasta Salad, 24
  Rotini Pasta Salad, 34
  Tuscan Salad, 27
salmon
  Baked Salmon with Olives, 139
  Italian-Style Salmon, 144
  Plum-Glazed Salmon with Polenta
    and Fried Leeks, 142–43
Sandberg, Ryne, 16, 75
sandwiches
  Chicken Parmigiana Sandwiches, 38
  Chicken Vesuvio Sandwiches, 43
  Grilled New York Strip Sirloin
    Sandwiches, 44
  Grilled Yellowfin Tuna (Ahi)
    Sandwiches, 39

Italian Beef Sandwiches Au Jus, 37
Italian Meatball Sandwiches, 46
Pepper-Crusted Beef Medallion
  Sandwiches, 45
Roasted Turkey Club Sandwiches, 42
sauces
  Aglio olio sauce (garlic and olive
    oil), pasta with, 111
  Alfredo Sauce, 83
  Arrabbiata Sauce, 84
  Aurore Sauce, 86
  Bordelaise Sauce, 93
  Caramel pecan sauce, chocolate
    tortas with, 192–93
  Cocktail Sauce, 89
  Hollandaise Sauce, 91
  Marinara Sauce, 81
  Meat Sauce, 82
  Parmigiano-Reggiano cream
    sauce, linguine with, 116–17
  Pesto Sauce, 85
  Pinot-Grigio butter sauce, yellowfin
    tuna with, 137
  Rémoulade Sauce, 87
  Roasted Red Pepper Cream Sauce, 88
  Vodka sauce, rigatoni with, 103
  White clam sauce, linguine with, 114
  Zabaglione, fresh berries with, 187
sausage
  Italian Sausage and Peppers, 129
  Marco Polo, 131
  Risotto with Italian Sausage and
    Leeks, 126
  Rotini with Italian Sausage, Fennel,
    and Portobello Mushrooms, 104
  Tuscan Bean and Sausage Soup, 8
Sautéed Broccoli and Mushrooms with
  Garlic, 76
Sautéed Mushrooms, 73
Sautéed Spinach with Garlic and Oil, 70
Savory Italian Cheese Platter, 50
scallops
  Saffron Risotto with Cremini
    Mushrooms, Asparagus, and
    Grilled Sea Scallops, 121
seafood
  Baked Clams, 55

seafood *continued*
Baked Grouper Oreganato, 141
Baked Salmon with Olives, 139
Broiled Australian Cold-Water
Rock Lobster Tails, 146
Chilled Lobster Salad with Garlic
Toast Points, 33
Fried Shrimp, 145
Grilled Halibut Fillet with Broccoli
and Chanterelle Mushroom
Risotto, 120
Grilled Marinated Octopus with
Spicy Infused Olive Oil, 51
Grilled Yellowfin Tuna (Ahi)
Sandwiches, 39
Italian-Style Salmon, 144
Jumbo Lump Crab Cakes, 52
Jumbo Shrimp Cocktail, 53
Linguine di Mare, 112
Linguine with Lemon-Garlic
Shrimp and Parmigiano-Reggiano
Cream Sauce, 116–17
Linguine with Red Clam
Sauce, 115
Linguine with White Clam
Sauce, 114
Mussels Marinara, 60
Mussels Steamed in Garlic, 61
Pan-Seared, Peppered Yellowfin
Tuna with Pinot Grigio Butter
Sauce, 137
Plum-Glazed Salmon with Polenta
and Fried Leeks, 142–43
Saffron Risotto with Cremini
Mushrooms, Asparagus, and
Grilled Sea Scallops, 121
Shrimp De Jonghe, 138–39
Shrimp Marsala, 62
Shrimp Scampi over
Capellini, 113
Surf and Turf, 181
Shallot butter with brandy, 90
shrimp
Fried Shrimp, 145
Jumbo Shrimp Cocktail, 53
Linguine with Lemon-Garlic Shrimp

and Parmigiano-Reggiano Cream
Sauce, 116–17
Linguine di Mare, 112
Shrimp De Jonghe, 138–39
Shrimp Marsala, 62
Shrimp Scampi over
Capellini, 113
side dishes
Creamed Spinach, 77
Garlic Mashed Potatoes, 71
Grilled Asparagus, 78
Homemade Italian Meatballs, 69
Sautéed Broccoli and Mushrooms
with Garlic, 76
Sautéed Mushrooms, 73
Sautéed Spinach with Garlic and
Oil, 70
Vesuvio Potatoes, 72
Smyth, John P., 172, 173
Sosa, Sammy, 41, 75, 173
soups
Cream of Zucchini Soup, 11
Creamy Potato and Pancetta
Soup, 14
Creamy Roasted Garlic Soup, 10
Homemade Beef Stock, 95
Homemade Chicken Stock, 94
Italian Onion Soup, 9
Minestrone Soup, 7
Potato and Onion Soup, 13
Tomato Basil Soup, 12
Tuscan Bean and Sausage Soup, 8
Spaghetti with Italian Meatballs, 110
spinach
Creamed Spinach, 77
Sautéed Spinach with Garlic and
Oil, 70
squid
Linguine di Mare, 112
St. Louis Cardinals, 2, 31, 40, 74
Steak, *See* beef
stock
Homemade Beef Stock, 95
Homemade Chicken Stock, 94
Stock Yards, 164
Stone, Steve, 4, 164

Stuffed Italian Pork Chops, 180
Stuffed Sweet Red Peppers, 134
Sun-Dried Tomato Vinaigrette, 96
Sundaes, hot fudge brownie, 186
Surf and Turf, 181
Sweet Herb Vinaigrette, 97
Sweet Italian Cheese Platter, 66
Sweet Potato and Wild Mushroom
Risotto, 119

T
"Take Me Out to the Ball Game," 1, 2,
4, 17, 41, 173
tomatoes
Beef Tenderloin Tips with Gorgonzola
Cheese and Roma Tomatoes, 182
Great Tomato, Onion, and Anchovy
Salad, 29
Sun-Dried Tomato Vinaigrette, 96
Tomato Basil Soup, 12
tuna
Grilled Yellowfin Tuna (Ahi)
Sandwiches, 39
Pan-Seared, Peppered Yellowfin
Tuna with Pinot Grigio Butter
Sauce, 137
Turkey club sandwiches, roasted, 42
Tuscan Bean and Sausage Soup, 8
Tuscan Bread Salad (Panzanella), 28
Tuscan Salad, 27

V
veal
Marco Polo, 131
Osso Buco, 132, 199
Veal Chops with Peppers and
Onions, 175
Veal Marsala, 174
Veal Parmigiana, 169
Veal Piccata, 170
Veal Scaloppine, 171
vegetables
Asparagus with Prosciutto and
Gorgonzola in Peppercorn
Vinaigrette, 63
Broccoli Salad, 32

vegetables *continued*
    Creamed Spinach, 77
    Eggplant Parmigiana, 130
    Garlic Mashed Potatoes, 71
    Grilled Asparagus, 78
    Roasted Red Peppers, 54
    Roasted Vegetable Risotto, 123
    Sautéed Broccoli and Mushrooms
      with Garlic, 76
    Sautéed Mushrooms, 73
Sautéed Spinach with Garlic and Oil, 70
    Stuffed Sweet Red Peppers, 134
    Sweet Potato and Wild Mushroom
      Risotto, 119
    Vesuvio Potatoes, 72
Vettel, Phil, 1–2, 149

vinaigrettes
    Asparagus with Prosciutto and
      Gorgonzola in Peppercorn
      Vinaigrette, 63
    Italian Vinaigrette, 100
    Raspberry Vinaigrette, 98
    Sun-Dried Tomato Vinaigrette, 96
    Sweet Herb Vinaigrette, 97

W
Ward, James, 149
Williams, Billy, 75
Williams, Ted, 74
Wood, Kerry, 75
Wrigley Field, xiii, 1, 18, 40–41, 74

Z
Zabaglione, fresh berries with, 187
ziti
    Baked Ziti, 107
    Ziti with Grilled Chicken and Pesto
      Sauce, 108
Zucchini soup, cream of, 11